PRAISE FOR
HERS FOR THE TAKING

Hers for the Taking outlines a treasure trove of insights and strategies for modern women as they navigate their professional and personal lives. Tracey offers practical and actionable advice that can be implemented across any career path, empowering readers to seize every opportunity that comes their way.

—Sheila Jordan
Senior Vice President, Chief Digital Technology Officer at Honeywell, Board Member, Author

Hers for the Taking lays out a clear path of success for the reader, along with so many powerful stories of trailblazing women who will entertain and inspire you to claim your own seat at the table in the C-Suite and beyond.

—Paula Hansen
President, Docusign, Board Member

Tracey has written a much-needed book. As opposed to those who study greatness and write academic theory, Tracey delivers much more. The simple, pragmatic steps this book takes, demystifies overpriced education and emphasizes the real stuff: guts, unrelenting work ethic, humility, coachability, and adaptability. This is a must read for my three adult daughters and, quite frankly, any professional who wants to own their outcome.

—Matt Sharrers
Managing Partner, ETJ Advisory, Chairman and Board Advisor

A powerful blueprint for women at all levels, this book will inspire, entertain, and accelerate your journey to the top, providing you with the wisdom, strategies, and practical tools to ensure a clear path to success.

—Heidi Melin
Board Member, C-Suite Executive, and Advisor

We need more women in the C-Suite, and *Hers for the Taking* is a must read for all women who aspire to reach their highest potential in their career.

—Stephanie Chung
Board Member, Global Speaker, C-Suite Executive, and Best-Selling Author of Ally Leadership: How To Lead People Who Are Not Like You

If you're looking to break through the glass ceiling, this book is for you. It is filled with stories and best practices to help you accelerate your rise to the boardroom, while inspiring you to be your best self along the way.

—Diane Adams
Board Member, C-Suite Executive, and Advisor

For those seeking to maximize their career potential, this book will serve as a practical playbook and road map. It is filled with inspiring stories and proven strategies that will help you fast-track your journey to the boardroom while motivating you to reach your full potential along the way.

—Debbie McClure
Global Head of Sales at Dropbox and Advisor

Throughout my career, I've worked with countless women and girls, and a recurring challenge I've seen is the lack of self-confidence in their abilities to succeed and advance. Tracey Newell's *Hers for the Taking* not only breaks down these barriers but also provides a clear, actionable road map. It shatters the illusion of limitations and empowers women from all backgrounds and education levels to rise above obstacles and reach their full potential.

—Kimberly Fay Boucher
MIT Senior Lecturer of Entrepreneurship, Cofounder of Women's Foundation of Boston, Technology Executive, and Board Advisor

Over the past twenty-three years I have had the privilege of watching Tracey's extraordinary career develop from an up-and-coming director of sales to a young vice president to a chief revenue officer to a company president and now to a board member of multiple companies. I could tell the first time I met Tracey, that she was destined to make a huge impact on not only the companies she helped lead, but a much larger audience as well. The thing that impresses me the most is that Tracey is the total package. In addition to her tremendous success in business, she is also an incredible mother and wife and one of the best human beings I know. She literally does it all! I mentioned to her years ago that she should write a book detailing how aspiring young women (and men) could model her path to success and now she has done it. If you aspire to play at the highest levels in business and life, Tracey's book will show you exactly how to do it and inspire you to actually go out and do it!

—Tom McCarthy
CEO, Founder, Executive Coach, and Author

HERS
FOR THE TAKING

TRACEY
NEWELL

HERS
FOR THE TAKING

YOUR PATH TO
THE C-SUITE
& BEYOND

Advantage | Books

Copyright © 2025 by Tracey Newell.

All rights reserved. No part of this book may be used or reproduced in any manner whatsoever without prior written consent of the author, except as provided by the United States of America copyright law.

Published by Advantage Books, Charleston, South Carolina.
An imprint of Advantage Media.

ADVANTAGE is a registered trademark, and the Advantage colophon is a trademark of Advantage Media Group, Inc.

Printed in the United States of America.

10 9 8 7 6 5 4 3 2 1

ISBN: 979-8-89188-251-5 (Hardcover)
ISBN: 979-8-89188-140-2 (Paperback)
ISBN: 979-8-89188-141-9 (eBook)

Library of Congress Control Number: 2024925184

Cover design by Lance Buckley.
Layout design by Ruthie Wood.

This publication is designed to provide accurate and authoritative information in regard to the subject matter covered. It is sold with the understanding that the publisher is not engaged in rendering legal, accounting, or other professional services. If legal advice or other expert assistance is required, the services of a competent professional person should be sought.

> Advantage Books is an imprint of Advantage Media Group. Advantage Media helps busy entrepreneurs, CEOs, and leaders write and publish a book to grow their business and become the authority in their field. Advantage authors comprise an exclusive community of industry professionals, idea-makers, and thought leaders. For more information go to **advantagemedia.com**.

To my parents, who always encouraged me to dream big, and then to get to work. And to my amazing husband. What a ride we have had together. I am eternally grateful for you.

CONTENTS

ABOUT THE AUTHOR..................XIII

CONTACT............................. XV

INTRODUCTION 1

PART ONE......................... 9

CHAPTER 1........................ 11
Take Charge of Your Own Career

CHAPTER 2........................ 19
To Lead or Not to Lead?

CHAPTER 3........................ 31
Career versus Family

CHAPTER 4........................ 43
Managing through Influence Is a Game Changer

PART TWO 53
Break Away from the Pack

CHAPTER 5 55
Set a High Bar

CHAPTER 6 65
Hire Your A-Team

CHAPTER 7 79
The Founder's Mindset

CHAPTER 8 87
The Power of Mentorship

CHAPTER 9 97
Tough Enough?

CHAPTER 10 111
Hitting a Ceiling

CHAPTER 11 121
Moving On

PART THREE 135
From Success to Significance

CHAPTER 12 137
Journey to the Boardroom

CHAPTER 13............................147
Leaving A Legacy

CHAPTER 14............................161
Faith and Your Career

CONCLUSION............................171

ACKNOWLEDGMENTS......................177

ABOUT THE AUTHOR

Specializing in accelerating go-to-market teams and top-line revenue growth, Tracey Newell has served on seven boards for high-growth software companies. Tracey also serves as an advisor for BlackRock Long Term Private Capital and Springcoast Capital Partners.

Tracey is the former president of Informatica, where she was a member of Informatica's board of directors for two years, prior to being asked to join Informatica's management team. As president of Informatica, Tracey was responsible for sales, marketing, revenue operations, and customer success.

Prior to joining Informatica, Tracey was EVP of global field operations at Proofpoint, where she led sales through a five-year period of hypergrowth from $100 million to $700 million. Recognized as a Top 100 Sales Leader by the Modern Sale, Tracey led Proofpoint's go-to-market team to become a top-five leader in the cybersecurity market. Before Proofpoint, Tracey was EVP of global sales at Polycom. She has also held sales leadership positions at Juniper Networks, Webex, and Cisco Systems. During her tenure at Cisco, Tracey was recognized by the organization Women Worth Watching.

From a philanthropic standpoint, Tracey is engaged with nonprofit Bridge2Rwanda (B2R), focused on building the next generation of African leaders; B2R Farms, which is focused on conservationist farming; and 4word, a Christian nonprofit focused on helping women to reach their God-given potential. Tracey graduated with honors from the University of California, Santa Barbara, and completed Stanford's twenty-sixth Annual Directors' College in June 2021.

CONTACT

To contact Tracey, learn more about her, or to access the free workbook that accompanies *Hers for the Taking*, scan the QR code below.

Our deepest fear is not that we are inadequate.
Our deepest fear is that we are powerful beyond measure.
It is our light, not our darkness, that most frightens us.
We ask ourselves, "Who am I to be brilliant, gorgeous, talented, fabulous?"
Actually, who are you not to be?[1]

---

1 Marianne Williamson, A Return to Love: Reflections on the Principles of a Course in Miracles (HarperOne, 1996).

INTRODUCTION

I almost wrote this book more than twenty-five years ago, as that was when I was planning to quit my job.

I was a second-line manager at Cisco, which was a Fortune 500 company at the time, managing a business worth hundreds of millions of dollars serving the public sector. I had been in the position for three or four years. We were doing well, which was part of the problem. A friend advised I had been branded the Queen of Public Sector, sharing that I was the only person in the company who could do what I did. My peers were telling me, "You'll never get out of this job," and I believed them. I felt trapped, and it was time for a career change.

I decided what I really wanted to do was write a book. I had been asked to do a lot of diversity work for my company at the time. When I started talking with my female colleagues about their experiences trying to build successful careers in tech, I was shocked. They were struggling with a long list of issues my male counterparts never gave a second thought to, including the following: *How can I get more people to listen to my ideas? How can I have my voice be heard when I'm the only woman on my team? How can I get to the next level? How can I balance family and work, and still have some semblance of a life?* I decided my book would address these issues. I'd strive to create a community where women could help each other, combined with practical advice and support. It would be the change I needed; it would get me out of my dead-end job; it would jump-start my new life.

But I never finished it.

And I didn't quit my job.

Instead, I went on to achieve things in my career that I had no idea were possible for someone like me, let alone for the women I hoped to advise. I had no idea what I didn't know. But now, after twenty-five years, I do.

Which is why I'm finally writing this book.

***

My name is Tracey Newell, and I am the former president of Informatica and have served on the board of directors for seven companies. I advise some of the greatest high-growth software companies in the world on how to scale. I lead what I consider a "life of influence" outside the office as well, serving as an advisor for the nonprofit Bridge2Rwanda while also on the board of a nonprofit known as 4word. I am a person who is deeply involved in my family and my community.

I am also a regular human being.

When I was starting out in the professional world, I watched the CEOs, board members, and management teams assemble in the conference room and wondered what secrets of the universe were being discussed behind those doors. In my mind, those people were from an entirely different class—they were not only more experienced than me but smarter and more talented in ways I couldn't even fathom. I was sure of it. Some of these people had probably known they would be running companies since kindergarten because their fathers, grandfathers, and great-grandfathers all ran companies. All of them were no doubt alpha dogs who got straight As at the best prep schools and Ivy

League universities before scoring their MBAs at Harvard, Stanford, or Yale. I assumed they were probably all ruthless and cutthroat and never saw their families … if they even had families. Their number one, two, and three priorities had to be their jobs.

I am living proof that none of that is true.

A friend of mine once said, "Tracey, you've completely ruined my faith in what it takes to be a senior executive, because you've shown me that anyone can do it." I started laughing (it was a joke, I promise), but there was a real kernel of truth in what my friend had shared. There is no driver's test to be a CEO. You have to really want the job, and then you have to earn the right through experience, hard work, and performance so that an executive team or board has confidence that you can do that job.

That's all there is to it.

My dad was a lawyer, and my stay-at-home mom had been a nurse, and each was the first of their family to go to college. I was an ordinary, middle-class, suburban-raised Northern California kid who went to public school. I did not work especially hard or achieve anything particularly noteworthy in high school. I did well enough to get into a good public university, but it wasn't UCLA or Berkeley. I did not go to grad school.

I do not have an MBA.

Obviously, never in my wildest imagination did I imagine a person like me could end up where I am today. But here I am. And if I had managed to finish that book or land another job, if I had walked away when I felt stuck instead of going deeper and pushing forward, I might still have no idea what I was capable of accomplishing.

And here's the thing. You might not know what you're capable of either.

I was lucky. I had some great advisors. With their help, I was able to imagine what a bigger future for myself might look like. I had the support I needed to make choices and take deliberate steps to bring that future to life.

This book is designed to give you support to do the same thing.

***

Then again, you might not want to do the same thing. Maybe, like thirty-five-year-old me, you assume these kinds of leadership roles are for "someone else," and you're fine with that assumption. But honestly, if not you, then *who*?

While you ponder this question, let me share a few quick statistics. According to a Catalyst study in 2022, women are indeed leaning into advanced degrees, exceeding men in bachelor's degrees, master's degrees, and doctorate degrees. Specifically, "In 2019–2020, women earned more than half of bachelor's degrees (57.7%), master's degrees (61.4%), and doctorate degrees (55.2%)."[2]

Now that sounds like really great progress, doesn't it? Yet, these amazing accomplishments are not translating into an increase of women in the C-suite at the rate you'd expect. The Equilar study from April of 2022 shared that with CNBC's TechCheck for women in the Russell 3000, women named executive officers increased from 8.1 to 13.7 percent by 2020, citing a 69 percent increase.[3] While 69.1 percent is a big increase from a percentage standpoint, these are still very small numbers given women make up more than 50 percent of the workforce.

---

[2] "Women in the Work Force: United States (Quick Take)," Catalyst, accessed September 30, 2024, https://www.catalyst.org/research/women-in-the-workforce-united-states.

[3] "Women in Executive Roles—A Reflection on the Last Decade," Equilar, accessed September 30, 2024, https://www.equilar.com/blogs/539-women-in-the-c-suite-last-decade.html.

In other words, we have a long way to go when it comes to representation in America's C-suites and boardrooms! And the reason is simple: Not enough of us are stepping up and choosing the path to senior leadership. There aren't enough of us in the pipeline, and that's a real problem—not because having more women in the boardroom is "the right thing to do," but because it's the smart thing to do. Study after study has proven that people do business with people who they relate to, who are *like them*. The studies show that the more diverse companies will have a competitive advantage among their competitors.

> According to a recent McKinsey report, the case for diversity continues to strengthen, with gender diversity on executive teams showing a 39 percent increase in financial outperformance.[4]

Beyond that, boardrooms are places where futures—not just of companies, but of all kinds of organizations—are determined. If women make up more than 50 percent of the population, we need to have more of a presence in the rooms where big decisions are being made. We need more women to choose a leadership trajectory and to provide the mentorship, support, and pathways that will make it easier for future generations to rise to the top.

This book is designed to help you be one of those women.

***

Think of this book as a blueprint to help you plot your career, step by step, so you ultimately finish in the C-suite or boardroom.

---

[4] The Power of Diversity: McKinsey's Latest Report Reinforces the Business Case for Inclusive Leadership," sunshowerlearning.com, November 18, 2024, https://sunshowerlearning.com/blog/the-power-of-diversity-mckinseys-latest-report-reinforces-the-business-case-for-inclusive-leadership.

We'll start with strategies to help you define your big-picture goals and deal with some of the misconceptions that may be holding you back and keeping you thinking small. You'll learn the difference between management and influence, how to become a person of influence, and how to find the right mentors and surround yourself with the right people to assist you on your journey. You'll get practical advice on what to do when you don't know how to balance work and family, when you don't get the promotion you want, when you're wondering if it's time to move on, and finally, what actually happens inside those boardrooms, and what to do when you get there. There will be exercises along the way to help you bring the process to life. We will also be celebrating many amazing women who have made it to the C-suite and beyond. These Transformational Leaders will share stories of how they handled some of the same challenges you may face and yet went on to build stellar careers.

> **Your choices today have the power to build a legacy for the women leaders of tomorrow.**

In the end, this book is about your leadership journey as well as how your individual efforts as a woman of influence can create a fundamental paradigm shift. Your choices today have the power to build a legacy for the women leaders of tomorrow. I'm here to tell you that this effort is worthwhile. You can do it, and I hope you will.

When I look back on what gave me the courage to say yes to leadership, I have a lot of mentors to thank, but I like to think it all started with my first role model: my father. My dad ingrained in me early in life that anything was possible. When faced with an impossible situation, he taught me I always had a choice. Would I accept a difficult situation or hardship, or would I work through it for the outcome I really wanted? There were always reasons but no excuses when it came to working through roadblocks in my family. His willingness to press me a bit further has always stuck with me. He taught me that if you really want to achieve something, you can.

I hope that in this book, I will tap you on the shoulder just like my dad and my mentors have tapped me, to tell you, "You can do this. You can do more."

Are you ready for the journey of your life? Then let's dive in.

PART ONE

I am very grateful for the many guides in my life who have encouraged me at different times to take a risk, to go for that next job, and who coached me to play the long game in thinking through my career goals holistically. I never dreamt I could lead a company, let alone do board work. And throughout this book, you will hear from many transformational women leaders who have also risen to the top of their organizations. My hope in part one of this book is to encourage you to take that next step in answering similar questions. If you were to dream a bit, what would you aspire to achieve in your career? Would you consider running a company? And can you do all these things while balancing work, family, and other priorities? If you're not sure, the next few chapters are for you.

CHAPTER 1

Take Charge of Your Own Career

Back when I was in my midthirties and miserable in my job, I had an hour-long meeting with my mentor. I walked into her office thinking, *I don't like my job, and I want a new one.* But I didn't tell her that.

Instead, I said, "I want to have more impact."

My mentor burst out laughing. She let out a laugh so hard and so loud I turned around and looked behind me to see if someone was making faces behind me. There wasn't.

She was laughing at *me*.

"Tracey," she said when I turned back around, "What does that mean? You want to have more impact? The head of janitorial services has impact. Do you want to do that? Do you want to be in charge of marketing? Do you want to run sales?"

Before I could answer, she said, "I could ask any man in this office that works for me what they want, and they will tell you exactly what they want to be. 'I'm going to be the CEO of a startup.' 'I'm going to run sales for this company.' 'I'm going to do this'; 'I'm going to do that.' Whether they actually do it or not, we'll never know. That story will be written later, but they can answer the question.

"So," she asked, "what do you want to do?"

"I don't know," I said. "I just know that I want to do something else."

"Like what?" she asked. "Do you want to run North America? Do you want to be a CEO?"

What was she, crazy? I was thirty-five with two kids under six years old! I couldn't fathom the idea of achieving such heights. I didn't know anyone who had run a company. So, I gave what I thought was the obvious answer: "No! I can't do any of those things!"

"Why not?" she asked.

I stated the obvious: "We're a twenty-billion-dollar company. How in the world could I do one of those big jobs?"

"Can you give me another reason?" she asked.

"Well," I said, "my kids are still so young. They're under six, and I'd never see them again. And I don't want to mess up my marriage ..."

"Okay," she continued. "How about in ten or fifteen years when your kids are in college? Would you run a company then?"

I honestly didn't know.

Would I ...?

Could I ...?

If my mentor hadn't asked me that question, I don't think I ever would have considered it. But the words "run a company" and "CEO" actually came out of her mouth in a conversation about *my* future. So, I thought about it. And when I did, I thought, *If I had the opportunity ...*

... well, maybe ...

So, I told my mentor that, yes, if I were to have the opportunity, I might be interested.

That's when she gave me the advice that really started the journey we're going to take in this book:

> "You need to plan your career *now* as if you were going to run a company ten or fifteen years from now so that you have the option when the time is right."

I wasn't exactly sure what she meant by that. As far as I was concerned, I had been planning my career. I was working very hard, beating my targets, pleasing my managers, getting promoted, all while raising two very young children with my husband. I often felt overwhelmed, juggling so many balls in the air, trying desperately to ensure none of them dropped. I couldn't think of anything I was *not* doing, to be perfectly honest. Then again, I was also unhappy and ready to leave my job, so whatever I was doing clearly wasn't working.

But why? What exactly was I missing?

The Twenty-First-Century Glass Ceiling

I believe that most men and women today start their careers in a similar way, in a similar place. They get on a path and go one step at a time, gradually assuming more responsibility, the way I did in my twenties and early thirties. However, while everyone starts out basically the same, the outcomes for men and women are still radically different. Why is the C-suite still close to 80 percent male? How can there still be a glass ceiling after we've spent decades working to shatter it?

The reality is that many women (and men) believe that one of several reasons for the lack of women in the C-suite comes down to a woman's ability to juggle both her family and her career.

However, if you dig a little deeper, the reality of the modern glass ceiling is more complicated. Research in the 2020 *Harvard Business Review* article "What's Really Holding Women Back"[5] suggests it's not the challenges of parenting but our culture of overwork that's to blame for stalling women's careers. Specifically, while men and women both struggle to manage their workloads, society pushes women to find "balance" via part-time or internally facing roles, which keeps them in the workforce but also slows or completely derails their career progression. Men, on the other hand, are not encouraged to seek "balance" but rather to work through the overwhelming situation and stay on track.

When Life Is Out of Balance

When you're exhausted and overwhelmed, all you want is for the world to stop spinning for five minutes, never mind to get eight hours of sleep. If your employer offers you *balance,* it can feel like you're drowning and someone just threw you a life preserver. It feels like safety. And deciding to start pursuing a path to the C-suite when you're exhausted and overwhelmed may sound … well, even more exhausting and overwhelming. But before you say, "not right now" or "this isn't for me," consider these two things:

1. Much of what you're afraid of when you think about what it takes to get to the C-suite are myths, and,

---

[5] Robin J. Ely and Irene Padavic, "What's Really Holding Women Back," *Harvard Business Review,* March–April 2020, https://hbr.org/2020/03/whats-really-holding-women-back.

2. Many of the issues you are currently facing will be very different fifteen, ten, even five years from now.

We'll take a deeper dive into some of those myths about women in leadership in the next chapter. For now, I want to zero in on the state of being overwhelmed. I think women fail to realize—and what I myself struggled with having two small children, trying to make a mortgage payment, being stressed about money, and feeling trapped in my job—is that being overwhelmed is a temporary state of being.

As a baby, one of my daughters was having trouble sleeping. When she was three months old, I was getting up every hour, all night long. Nothing I did could placate her, I was sure I was doing something wrong—and I was overwhelmed and exhausted. At the time you were allowed to call the nurses in the hospital, as there was always someone in the delivery room to give advice, and so I did. A nurse answered, and I broke down sobbing. "I don't know what's wrong," I told her.

"Honey," the nurse advised, "I don't know too many five-year-olds that are getting up every thirty to forty-five minutes. This is just a point in time, and it is going to pass."

It was like the clouds parted. I literally pulled the phone away from my ear and stared at it and thought,

It's not going to be like this forever.

It works the same way in our careers. It is easy to feel stuck, overwhelmed in the moment, and shift into survival mode. But if you don't take a second to pause when you're twenty-five, thirty, or thirty-five years old to think about the future, to think about what you really want to be doing a decade or two down the road, you're never going to get there. Just trudging along will get you paid, and it may even get you promoted. Maybe you'll even find balance. But it will not get you to the C-suite. For that, you need to make deliberate choices that will keep you moving forward on a leadership path.

Taking the Plunge

Of course, if you're going to make a plan to get somewhere, you need to know where you're going. That in itself can be a challenge—most people can't answer the question "What do you want to be doing in five years?" let alone ten or fifteen years. But getting to the C-suite is a long-term journey, and for that, you need to spend time on long-term planning. I want to stress that it is important to understand that you aren't going to figure this out in a day.

A lot of people want to be like Moses, where you head up the hill and march back down with your tablets containing your "Instructions for Life." Life doesn't work that way. A lot of this process will come down to embracing the art of the possible, and that starts with self-reflection. For me that meant reading a ton of books; for you it might be meditating, walking in nature, talking to your peers, or simply blocking out time to think. The idea is to give yourself permission to open your mind, to be bold and dream about something big. Ask yourself what you really want to be doing long term. Is your goal to remain in your current functional role, and if not, what role do you want to try? If you like what you're doing, is your goal to be the head of your function? Is it to manage managers? Be a vice president?

At a young age, I was fascinated by the author Napoleon Hill, who wrote *Think and Grow Rich*. As the story goes, Mr. Hill was hired as a young reporter to interview some of the most successful people in the world at that time, with the intent to write a book on how others could achieve similar success. One of the ideas I've never forgotten was that most people actually do get what they want in life ... but they set their sights too low. A new car, a new job, or a new home. I've seen the power of human potential and have come to appreciate that as Hill writes, "If you can conceive it, you can achieve it." How far would you go if there were no limits in your career? What's the biggest, most audacious thing you can imagine yourself doing?

Map Your Path to Success

Once you have set your sights on your big role, it's as simple (or, okay, not so simple) as reverse-engineering a path that will take you from where you want to go all the way back to where you are now.

So where do you start? Begin talking to the people around you, getting to know people in some of those higher-level roles you hope to obtain someday, understanding what their job is like and what a typical day consists of. For example, if you want to "run marketing" someday for your company, what are the chief marketing officer's roles and responsibilities? What are some of the shortfalls you currently have today against those requirements, and what can you do to plug those gaps over time? What experiences and other roles will you need to take on over the next five to ten years? I want you to literally start backing into a multiyear career plan.

Now that you've mapped out your long-term goal, let's go back to where you are today. You are going to climb this corporate ladder one step at a time, so what would be the logical next step in your current career path that gets you closer to your goal? What are the requirements for this role? What are your current gaps to landing your next promotion? As you establish your short-term target, think about how you can differentiate yourself today with the job you're currently in to ensure the next promotion is naturally yours. What would an amazing result be for your current job? Have you communicated to your boss and their boss that you want the next promotion? Could you take on a special project for your boss's boss that solves a real problem in your organization? And if you solve that problem, how would it differentiate you for the next promotion?

To make sure you don't slip back into survival mode, keep your eye on the big picture. At least once a year, make sure you are looking at your recent career decisions, checking in to ensure you are moving toward your long-term goal. And never lose sight of the fact that this is your career, and your life. I was once told, "No one can manage your career but you." These are words to live by, so I'd encourage you to aim high.

In our next chapter, we'll dive a little deeper into what it really means (and doesn't mean) to be a leader in the workplace.

CHAPTER 2

To Lead or Not to Lead?

Early in my career, my then-boss told me what he thought was very good news. "Hey," he said, "I put you up for a vice president role." In a Fortune 100 company, that's a big deal, especially for someone in their midthirties, which I was at the time.

My response to him was instantaneous. "Oh, no, that's okay. I like working for you. I don't need a promotion right now." (Really? Who turns down a vice president role!)

My boss looked at me, confused. "Tracey," he said, "you could truly have a good run if you simply got more serious about your career …"

I realize that might sound like he was being critical, but I knew that he wasn't. In that moment, my boss was trying to be a friend. He was genuinely curious. Why did I keep turning down the kind of opportunities that most people—in his mind, and I imagine in most *sane* people's minds—would kill for?

To me, the answer was obvious. It was the same answer I had given my previous mentor, who laughed at me when I told her I wanted to "have more impact." My honest answer was that I was the mother of two young kids! If I took an executive role, I'd be traveling 80 percent of the time, and I would never see my family again. A promotion simply wasn't worth risking my family!

I genuinely believed this all to be true.

But it wasn't; it was just a story I was telling myself. Something many professional women do all the time.

The Tales We Tell

We all tell ourselves stories. It's completely normal to run potential scenarios in your head around possible outcomes when you take any kind of risk. That's how we weigh pros and cons and make decisions. But often, women take this sort of storytelling to a destructive level that men do not, at least in our professional lives. The stories we tell ourselves about why we can't do things can often morph from fiction to facts in our minds. They become the things we "know" to be true, when they're really just stories.

A brilliant thirty-year-old woman I mentor recently called me for advice. Her boss had told her, "Hey, good news: I'm getting promoted, and I think you should take my job. I think you should become a manager." My immediate reaction was to say, "That's great! I'm so excited for you." Her reaction was a bit less enthusiastic.

"Well, I don't know," she said. "Is this the right thing for me?"

She had a million questions and a million reasons not to take this job. "Do you think I would be a good manager? What if I'm too busy right now? I'm already so busy. I'm getting married. Can I juggle it? Maybe I should wait. Maybe this isn't the right time." And on and on …

I had to laugh. It was like listening to myself when I was in my thirties, turning down an exec role for the umpteenth time because I was afraid that I could not be a great mom and a great executive simultaneously. In the decades since that conversation with my mentor, I've hired a lot of people and seen a lot of job descriptions, and not once have I seen one that read, "If you take this executive role, you'll have to travel 80 percent of the time and you'll never see your family again." I also know from personal experience that being an executive means you have *more* control over your life, not less.

So, I laughed, the way so many people have laughed with me, and told my mentee, "When your boss calls you back, you're going to say, 'Thank you so much. I've thought about it, and I want that job, and I'm going to crush it.' That's what you're going to say to your boss."

The reality is there are hundreds of possible outcomes to a promotion that do not include "I will never see my children again" or "I will lose control of my life." There are outcomes where you learn and grow and have incredible experiences and make a real impact on people's careers and lives. I know, because that's what happened to me. So why don't we tell ourselves *those* stories—the ones where we take the job and we succeed beyond our wildest imagination?

What in the world is stopping us?

Women and Imposter Syndrome

We all question our capabilities at one point or another in our lives. There are always moments when we ask ourselves, *Can I really do this?* We wonder if we're faking it more than we're actually making it. But imposter syndrome has done actual damage to the quest for gender equity in the C-suite. According to a study by the National Bureau of Economic Research, "close to 80 percent of women struggle with low self-esteem and shy away from self-advocacy at work. That means almost *four out of five women* may be held back in their career advancement by a lack of confidence and visibility."[6]

Sheryl Sandberg's Lean In Foundation[7] provides a painfully clear picture of what this phenomenon looks like. She shares a study of gender and race representation in the corporate space, with these descriptions going from highest to lowest: white men; men of color; white women; and finally, women of color.

Clearly, we have a pipeline problem, where we can see that more and more women are dropping out at every level. For many reasons, women reach a certain level in their careers, then say, "That's it," and they stop.

I remember a time when I had taken a job running sales for a CEO, fully intending, within a few years, to become a CEO. I was so confident I had shared my plan with my new boss from the get-go, and he agreed he was on Team Tracey. In other words, I walked in there telling myself the right kind of story. I was going to kill it. I was CEO bound.

Fast-forward one or two years, and my CEO asked, "Are you still planning to take on a CEO role?"

I hesitated. "I do want to," I stammered, "but in order to be ready, I really feel like I need to be better on the financials when speaking to investors. Of course I can read a P&L, but when talking to investors, I feel like I need to improve here …"

---

[6] Danielle Littlejohn, "What's Holding Women Back? Crises of Confidence in the Workplace," *Global Government Forum*, December 11, 2023, https://www.globalgovernmentforum.com/whats-holding-women-back-crises-of-confidence-in-the-workplace.

[7] "Women in the Workplace Study," Lean In, 2023, https://leanin.org/women-in-the-workplace?gad_source=1&gclid=CjwKCAjwx-CyBhAqEiwAeOcTdZOzaaazXvSTE-QOB5C65ClCvs941wt10HAgMnumc7GY-2fhI-J5VlxoC1SAQAvD_BwE.

My boss stopped me and smiled. "Tracey," he said, "you've run a P&L for ten plus years. What you're describing is the CFO's job. You don't have to be the CFO; you just have to hire a great CFO."

Even senior executives on the brink of getting everything they have ever wanted can *still* tell themselves the wrong stories. I am living proof.

Perception versus Reality

So, clearly, we have a problem. For whatever reason, we are wired to doubt ourselves, at least to some degree. We can acknowledge that and not beat ourselves up about it, but we also need to get past it if we're ever going to rise to our potential. Luckily, I have a solution: facts.

In my experience, the best way to counteract fiction—in this case those stories we tell ourselves about why we can't do things—is by hitting back with some cold, hard facts. Instead of letting false assumptions about the scary things a leadership role will require you to do *(or why you'll never be good enough or smart enough)* hold you back, why not find out for yourself exactly

1. What the specific role you're interested in actually entails
2. What your current skills are and where there are gaps you can work on

The best place to start is by taking inventory of the requirements of the job you aspire to obtain. If you want to lead a company someday, you're going to need these baseline qualities:

- C-suiters are thought leaders—individuals who have different ideas about how they can help their organization, their customers, their employees.

- They're very strong at strategy and planning.
- They're the best at building and developing strong teams.
- They are results oriented, execute consistently, and can be counted on to get things done.
- They're problem solvers in their own function but also cross-functionally think above and beyond outside their group. They think about the broader company.
- They have strong executive communication and public speaking skills.

If you want to be in the C-suite, those are all examples of requirements for that role.

And yes, I realize you may be reading that list and thinking, *But I'm not able to do* any *of those things well today!*

Before you panic (and plan to drop out and start writing your own book), remember, very few people start out as the CEO in their first job. They start developing those skills at much lower levels, in the roles they start out in—roles very much like the one you're probably in right now. What sets them apart and puts them on the senior leadership track is the way they approach those roles. Of course they make sure to master their current role with excellence. But they also clearly voice their desire to do the next role and—here's the crucial part—start demonstrating that they can do that *next role* while in their *current role*. Then they repeat the process for the next job, and the one after that, and the one after that … all the way to the C-suite.

It's just like learning to play a sport or mastering a hobby—you start out as the new person, perhaps confused, nervous, or overwhelmed, but as you stick with it, learn, and build your capacity over time, your skills grow. You keep looking for the next challenge, tackling it, and moving on to the next one, until you're an expert.

So, start small. Ask yourself, *What would it take to be stellar in my boss's role, or my boss's boss's role?*

If you aspire to be in management, my advice is to simply start practicing the art of management in your current role. You don't need an official title to help guide a peer or someone who may be new to their position. Reaching out with an olive branch to help mentor others is a great way to develop management skills. (And anyone you help along the way will surely be rooting for you when the next promotion comes up!)

Another great way to be recognized as a leader, and my personal favorite, is to be known as the problem solver. If something isn't working for your team, why not tell your manager you'd like to work on that issue? I can almost guarantee they'll say yes. Problem solving is a big piece of leading—if you are able to demonstrate to your boss and their boss that you're someone who drives change, at the end of the day, that is what the executives are here to do for your company. They set strategy to help your company differentiate and accelerate growth, and they deliver results for shareholders. The earlier you start modeling this behavior, the faster you'll shoot to the top.

Filling in the Gaps

Once you understand the skills that you will need for that bigger job, you can inventory your strengths as they relate to those behaviors and pinpoint the weaknesses you need to work on. For example, if you're not comfortable with public speaking, think of three things you can work on this year that will help you get more comfortable in front of a microphone. You could join an organization like Toastmasters, volunteer to do a speech at one of your sessions, get a coach, take a class ... It's not about bridging all these gaps in a week or a year, it's about taking steps to get you closer to your long-term goals.

So, take a look at the jobs that are a few levels above you and identify what the gaps are and also what you will need to do to bridge them. Once you know what you need to do, it's just a matter of breaking it down into steps, like we discussed in the last chapter. And as I have learned, if you can do this for your next job, then you can do this for three jobs up. My target was always to think two levels above where I was at the time. Of course, my first priority was to be exceptional in my current role, but I also worked to model those next levels' requirements while in my current job.

With this thought in mind, I want to address the overused corporate term known as "managing up." I can't tell you the number of times men and women (at all levels) explained to me what a bad job they do at "managing up." They would share stories of their peers who were constantly bragging to the leadership team about "all the great things that they were doing," and that, for whatever reason, they couldn't be those people. I always corrected them on the definition of "managing up." This phrase implies you are being manipulative, or perhaps you are singing your praises for your own benefit, not the company's benefit. I don't actually see the people who are truly doing great things for the company and then sharing those things with their boss as "managing up."

I am looking for leaders at all levels who have figured out how to solve complex problems that exist inside the company, and who are also willing to share how they are getting their results. Those leaders will come to me and say, "I figured out how to solve this problem—can I tell you about it?" These change agents allow me to take whatever problem they've solved and scale their solution throughout the company. Because of what they have done (and shared), the entire company can go faster.

In the end, leaders are driven people who get things done. Great leaders are passionate about what they do. They create a mission and strategies for their team. They identify roadblocks and remove them. If you do this in whatever role you're in, you will win the hearts and minds of your team, and you'll be unstoppable. That's the kind of story you should be telling yourself, and the kind of story that will take you to the top, like Heidi Melin.

TRANSFORMATIONAL LEADER: HEIDI MELIN, BOARD MEMBER AND ADVISOR

Heidi Melin is a strategic marketing leader, board director, and GTM (go-to-market) advisor with three decades of senior marketing leadership experience and a reputation for building award-winning marketing teams in the technology industry. Most recently Heidi was the CMO of Workfront, a leader in enterprise work management, acquired by Adobe in January, 2021, and she previously served as CMO of Plex Systems, Eloqua, Polycom, Taleo, and Hyperion and was group vice president of marketing at PeopleSoft. She is also an experienced board director for both public and privately held companies and currently serves as an independent board director for Origami Risk.

***

I was a senior executive at a software company where I'd been for almost ten years. I came in as a director, was promoted to VP level, and then into a group VP level. Then, at a pivotal moment, we faced a hostile takeover. The next nineteen months were a phenomenal experience that I never want to repeat. But it gave me the opportunity to leave my company, which I probably wouldn't have done otherwise, and to think about what was next. Very shortly I had a CMO opportunity at a public company with about $750 million in revenue. And I was terrified. I'd never sat in a C-suite; I'd never been a 16(b) officer. I was thirty-eight and had young children, and the job involved a commute, travel—all of the things. But the CEO of this company had more confidence in me than I had in myself. I decided that there was a reason why he believed in me, and I needed to rise to the challenge. I took the risk, and (almost) every day I was glad that I did. I'm not going to lie; there were a couple of days when I thought, Why did I do this? But make no mistake—it was this decision that was foundational to the rest of my career.

My advice for making your own leap to the C-Suite is as follows:

1. **Invest in key relationships.** *Spend time cultivating the relationships in your network. I don't mean the connections you have on LinkedIn. I'm talking about relationships that you have spent time building, where if the person needs something, you're there, and if you need something, they're there. When I look back at my career holistically, those relationships are what helped catapult me forward.*

2. **Take risks.** *But, don't just use your own gut as your guide. I am not a natural risk-taker at all, but I have people in my personal and professional life who are thrilled to support me in those risks. I might assess the risk level of something and say, "This is terrify-*

ing, I'm never going to do it," and my husband will say, *"Why not?" It's okay to lean on other people to push yourself forward.*

3. **Remember that work-life balance is not a destination.** *Balance is a constant state of motion. For example, I was traveling and missed my daughter's first day of kindergarten. Which was also her birthday. I felt awful, but my husband said, "You can go on the third day, and parking won't be as challenging." I did, and he was right on both fronts. And, twenty-five years later, my daughter doesn't even remember!*

What will your day-to-day life look like when you reach the C-suite? In the end, that's entirely up to you. I certainly know and have worked with people who live to work instead of working to live. And I'll be honest, there are times when work has taken up 100 percent of my life. But there are also times when life has required 100 percent, and I have given it. I want to be clear—I worked very hard as an operating executive and expected the same from my team. There were dinners, nights, weekends; it was all part of the job. But if something was important at home, I made sure I was home. Knowing your priorities in life is critical, and ensuring you have balance for what matters is key, which we'll discuss in the next chapter.

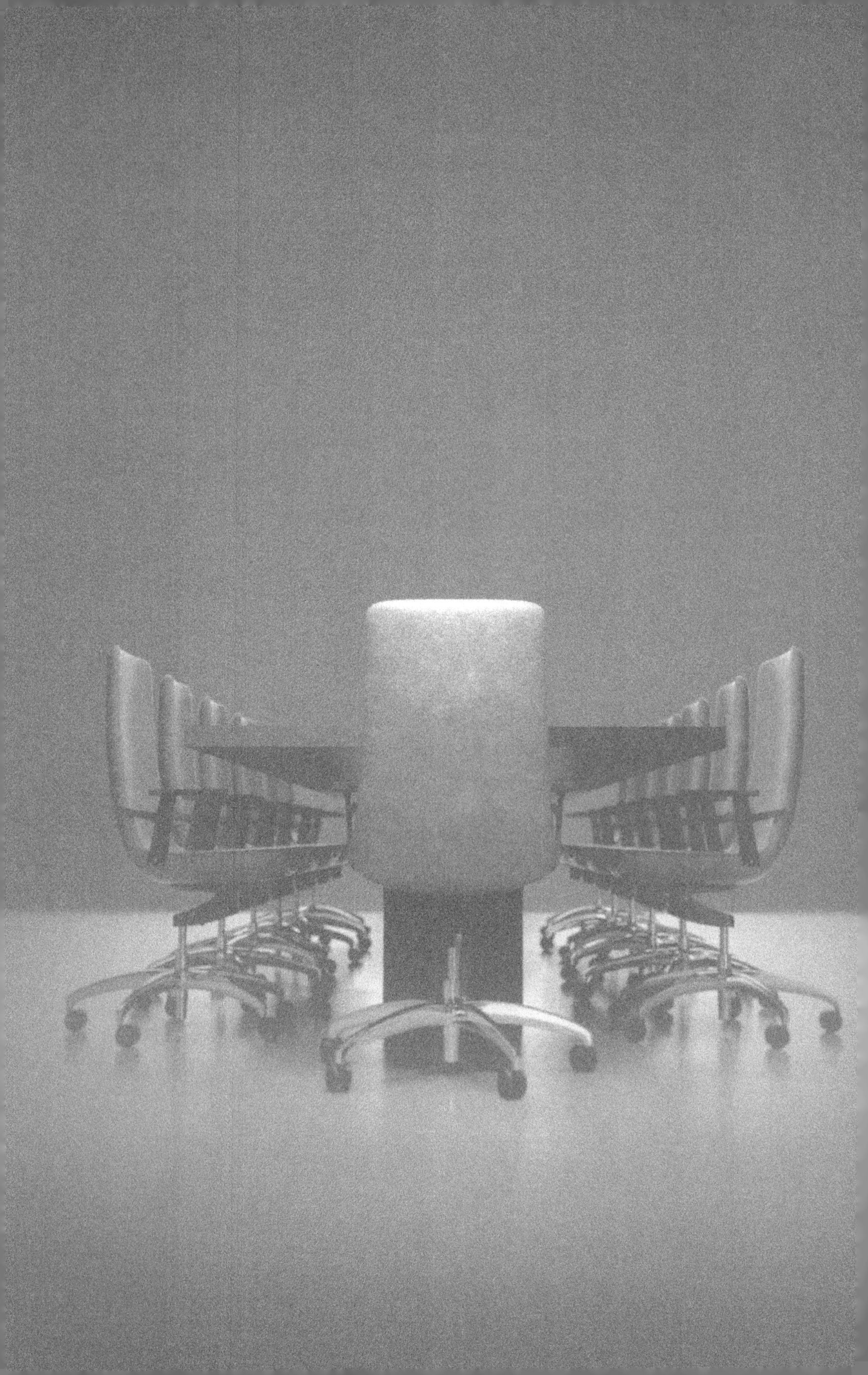

CHAPTER 3

Career versus Family

In my early thirties, when I was a second-line manager, I attended a conference in Arizona. I was chatting with a colleague and asked her, "How's it going?"

"I'm enjoying the conference, but I miss my son," she said.

"Oh, I know," I replied. "It's so hard traveling with little kids at home."

Our boss overheard our conversation and said, "I don't understand. What's the problem?"

"We feel bad," I told him. "We want to be perfect moms at home raising our kids, and we want to be perfect at work. We want to do all those things, and it's impossible to balance our lives."

"I don't get it," he said. "I have four kids, and I'm providing for them. Most of the world's population is struggling to put food on the table, and I'm giving my kids a good life and showing them that they can work hard and do great things too."

He went on and on, and I kept thinking about it afterward. Why was he so *comfortable*?

And then it hit me. He was choosing *not* to feel guilty about his choices to excel in his career.

Fast-forward to a week later. I was taking my daughter to kindergarten, and she asked me, "Mom, how come you're not like the other moms? You don't make brownies, you don't help with homework, you don't help with math in my classroom."

If this had happened a month ago, I would have been devastated. But in thinking through that conversation with my boss, I decided to *choose* not to feel guilty. Without even thinking, I answered her, "You know what? There are all kinds of moms out there. Some of them work inside the home, and some of them help in the classroom every day. Those are amazing jobs. And then there are other moms that work outside the home, and that's what I do. And I'm really good at my job, and I really like it. It is an important job. And because of it we get to live in our house, pay our bills, and sometimes go on fun vacations." I dropped her off and forgot all about the conversation.

> **The people around us just want us to be happy with our choices and to be present when it matters.**

A week later, I was driving her to school again, this time with two of her little friends in the back seat with her. I overheard my little five-year-old explain to two other five-year-olds, "Well, my mom's got a really big job, and she's really good at her job, and she leads all of these people." I couldn't believe it! I had a true "aha" moment:

The people around us just want us to be happy with our choices and to be present when it matters.

I believe the key in life is to do both.

You *Can* Have It All ... If You Redefine "All"

Ever since legendary *Cosmopolitan* editor-in-chief Helen Gurley Brown published the iconic self-help missive *Having It All,* professional women have been striving to attain this almost mythical state of perfect work-life balance. It didn't take long for research to prove they were chasing something that didn't exist. A 2002 *Harvard Business Review* study concluded that, thirty years after the women's movement, female executives "still don't have it all, and probably never will."[8] A decade later, in 2012, *The Atlantic* said that women trying to "have it all" were "fooling themselves."[9] And just last year, in 2023, *The Guardian* theorized that "Having it all is a myth used to punish working mothers."[10]

Close to fifty years since the phrase first entered the lexicon, the prevailing viewpoint today is that "having it all" is impossible, at least until systemic changes remove the structural barriers that are holding women back. That means offering things like flexible working conditions, affordable childcare, and parental leave.[11] I agree that all these things are very necessary and can and will make a tremendous difference

---

[8] Sylvia Ann Hewlett, "Executive Women and the Myth of Having It All," *Harvard Business Review,* April, 2002, https://hbr.org/2002/04/executive-women-and-the-myth-of-having-it-all.

[9] Anne-Marie Slaughter, "Why Women Still Can't Have It All," *The Atlantic,* July/August 2012, https://www.theatlantic.com/magazine/archive/2012/07/why-women-still-cant-have-it-all/309020/.

[10] Antoinette Latouffe, "'Having It All' Is a Myth Still Being Used to Punish Working Mothers," *The Guardian,* February 14, 2023, https://www.theguardian.com/commentisfree/2023/feb/14/having-it-all-is-a-myth-still-being-used-to-punish-working-women.

[11] "Covid 19 and Gender Equality: Countering the Regressive Effects," McKinsey, July 15, 2020, https://www.mckinsey.com/featured-insights/future-of-work/covid-19-and-gender-equality-countering-the-regressive-effects.

in growing the pipeline and getting more women into the C-suite, but that doesn't mean there's nothing you can do while we're waiting.

Maybe your workplace isn't ideally structured to support your life as a working parent. Few workplaces are. I don't in any way want to belittle the struggles of working mothers. I see you. I have *been* you, and I am fully aware that sometimes your life is going to feel impossible. But I also know you will get through it, and if you're going to be a working mother anyway, you might as well turn off the guilt and be the best working mom you can be. And the good news is, you get to define what that means. It doesn't have to be all or nothing—you can have a great career and also have an amazing relationship and family, however you define it. You can be a fabulous mother, daughter, sister—fill in the blank. It's a matter of framing your choices in terms of what you can do rather than what you can't.

Too often, we worry about what we can't do. Even before I had my sights set on the C-suite, I always knew that I wanted to be outstanding at my job, but at the same time, there was nothing more important to me than my friends, family, and faith. I wasn't sure there was room in my life for all those priorities. You assume something has to give, right?

Then I took a class based on Stephen Covey's *Seven Habits of Highly Effective People.* One exercise really resonated with me: There was this huge bowl, a bunch of rocks, and a big bag of sand. The guy leading the class took the bag of sand and poured it into the bowl. Then he asked the class to start putting the rocks, each of which represented a life priority like career or family or faith or health, into the bowl, one at a time. Everyone took turns calling out things that were important to them. Somebody called out "career," and that rock went in. Somebody else said "family," and that rock went in. Someone else said "working out," and someone else said "my friends." Pretty soon the bowl was full, and there were three or four rocks, all of which also represented very important priorities to a lot of people, just sitting there.

We assumed the point of the exercise was to demonstrate that it was impossible to "have it all." If we were going to have the things we wanted most in life, we would have to give up other things that mattered to us to make room.

But then the leader flipped the script. He took everything out of the bowl, put the rocks back on the table, the sand back in the bag. Then he started over, but this time, we put the big important rocks in the bowl first, one by one. They all fit. Then he took the bag of sand and poured it all out over the top of the rocks. It filtered down through the bowl, leaving the rocks undisturbed. It turned out there was room for everything.

The leader explained that the sand represented the noise in life. It's all those emails, all the texts, the hundred things on the to-do list that matter, but if you get them done tomorrow or the next day, it'll probably be fine. Covey's point was clear and obvious. You need to have priorities, and you need to put yourself on the list to ensure you work through the things that matter most first. I think that's timeless advice.

Your Calendar Is Your Lifeline

If you're going to advance in your career, one of the first rocks that goes in your bowl needs to be a winning strategy. And most people simply don't make time to build a real strategy. In writing. Why? "My job is overwhelming. I'm doing emails six hours a day." When I hear this, I'll reply, "Well, then you're not doing your job very well." Sounds a little tough, I know, but sometimes tough love is necessary. It's also why God gave us calendars.

Even though I'm pseudo-retired, my calendar is still my life. If I need to do something, it goes on my calendar, whether it's a meeting or buying my husband a birthday gift, and that's how I make sure the important things happen. Period. Since having a breakthrough strategy was critical in every role I ever had, it went on my calendar too.

For example, when I felt myself getting overwhelmed with all the noise and losing focus, I would take out my calendar and schedule two hours to work on strategy the next Monday. If that time needed to get moved for a critical meeting, that was fine, but once it went on the calendar, that meant I had to get it done *that week*. No excuses. When I put the things that mattered on my calendar, I could not *not do* what mattered in my life, personally or professionally. If there was an important school play, I'd put it on my calendar, and nothing could get in the way of me attending the play. I wanted to be home for birthdays, and so I put those on my calendar, too, and I was home for almost every birthday.

I also use my calendar to keep myself on track toward my goals. During that Monday strategy session, I would think about the most important things I wanted to accomplish that week, that month, that quarter, and put them all on the calendar. I don't limit this scheduling to professional items but also use it for personal activities, like meeting a friend I've been neglecting or going to the gym. I know that if I just hope I'm going to get to it, and it's not on the calendar, it's not going to happen. So, I make sure it does.

At the end of the day, you are in charge of your schedule. Maybe you can't have it all, but you can have what matters to you by knowing your priorities, scheduling them, sticking to them, and allowing yourself to be comfortable with your choices.

Which takes me back to Covey's rocks. Whether it's friends, or family, or faith, or fitness *(or even something that doesn't start with an f)*, put that rock in the bowl first by putting it on your calendar, making it just as important as the things you have to get done for your job. Schedule your own block of time to work on your critical initiatives for the month or the quarter before you deal with the emails and the phone calls and the rest of the noise. At the same time, don't let your calendar take advantage of you. You own your calendar—it does not own you!

Also keep in mind that as you move into more executive roles, you really are going to have more control over where and how you spend your time. I don't think I understood that when I was in my thirties and worried that an executive position would basically destroy my life. The first time I took a job at that level, I suddenly realized: *No one's making me travel anywhere. As an executive, it's my job to decide what's important. And if it's important, then I jump on a plane. But traveling for traveling's sake isn't part of the job.*

In the end, you get to decide where you spend your time—as long as you're excelling in your job. Excellence always has to come first if you're aiming for a spot in the C-suite. But after that, there's time in your life for all the things that matter to you. And there's no need to apologize for doing the things you need to do in your life.

I'm on a personal mission to get women to stop apologizing. We often say "I'm sorry" in circumstances where men would not. For example, I was recently mentoring a senior woman at the SVP level who had to leave a meeting early. The executive team was running thirty minutes late, and she had to go. She explained, "I'm a single mom and I'm so sorry, but I need to leave. I'm the only one who can pick up my child." She kept on apologizing and explaining for a while. When she finally stopped, I said, "Okay, don't ever do that again."

"Do what?" she asked.

I said, "A man would've said, 'Hey guys, sorry I have a hard stop at five.' They would say that an hour before the meeting is scheduled to end. They'd say, 'I have a hard stop at five, we're running late, so what do we need to get through today?' Their hard stop might be meeting someone for dinner, it might be watching their son play baseball, but that is not the point. The point is that the meeting was to conclude at five p.m., and they're not going to apologize for leaving on time. And they most likely won't even tell you what is causing the hard stop." Pro tip: you don't have to either!

As I've said before, you do have to be good at your job. But once that's handled, the rest of your time is yours. Your boss doesn't care if you work until 5:30 p.m. every evening. Your boss wants you to be exceptional at your job.

So don't worry so much about whether you can "have it all." If you identify your priorities and hold yourself to them as much as you can, you can have what matters to you—including a great career—on your terms. I'm not the only woman I know who has done this. This book is full of women who have had amazing careers and are also amazing moms and wives ... like the amazing woman you're about to meet.

TRANSFORMATIONAL LEADER: KARA WILSON, FORMER CMO, BOARD DIRECTOR AND EXECUTIVE ADVISOR

A board director and advisor to both large corporations and technology startups in the United States and Europe, Kara Wilson has over thirty years of experience driving go-to-market strategies for some of the most influential companies in the industry. She has served as executive vice president and chief marketing officer at Okta, SAP Cloud, FireEye, Rubrik, Success Factors, and Network General. She has held senior marketing leadership positions at Cisco and PeopleSoft and is currently an executive advisor for KKR. Kara has launched brands, created categories, navigated hyper growth through IPO, and is passionate about redefining the traditional approach to marketing. She is currently a board director at Paychex (PAYX), OneStream (OS), ReliaQuest, OutSystems, and Alludo.

***

Did you ever see the movie I Don't Know How She Does It? *about a working mom trying desperately to balance her career and her family and failing spectacularly? Back in my thirties when my kids were small, the star of this movie was me. During one of my particularly low points, my six-year-old daughter tried to flush my cell phone down the toilet. As I dug my phone out of the toilet in tears, my husband laughingly said, "Well,* that was a clear message." There were times when I was gone too often, and everyone was frustrated with me when I needed to take a nap after arriving home from a week in China. I regret that there were not enough real conversations about what we were trying to accomplish together as a team, as a couple, and as a family.

I wish someone would've told me it's okay to be out of balance at times—that being a good parent and partner can be pretty messy most of the time, so give yourself grace. People talk about work-life balance, but I think that's a pipe dream, it's really about work-life integration. Don't fool yourself, as it's a tricky dribble, and you need a great partner to meet you halfway. When things begin to wobble, know there's light at the end of the tunnel. Life can be messy, but it's a point in time, and you will get through it.

My advice to survive the messy times is this:

1. **Communicate, communicate, communicate**: *Be honest and vulnerable with your partner and your kids. Don't complain, but be honest when you need help. It's okay to tell your kids, "Hey, I'm really sorry that I've been so busy, but I'm working very hard so that we can have the things we need, and we will have more fun soon." Kids understand honest communication, and when they feel like they're part of the solution, they're in it to win it with you.*

2. **Plan ahead:** *Your family, your partner, or whoever is on your team needs the exact data regarding the plan for the month. For example; "I'm traveling this week. I'm going to come home on this day. I'm going to be tired, and I will probably need to nap, so please try to understand I'm on an eighteen-hour time difference."*

3. **Put yourself on the list:** *When you're climbing the ladder, it's hard to find moments for yourself, and yet it's the most important thing to do. Even though you may feel a bit guilty when you're taking time to do something that's just for you, you're going to be a better mom if you're calm.*

At the end of the day, being ambitious in your career does not mean saying no to everything and everyone else you love. Make time for what matters to you personally as well as professionally and be proud of your accomplishments in both realms. I truly believe it's what the people who love you want for you. In the next chapter, we'll turn our focus to making those accomplishments happen when we look at the differences between influence and management.

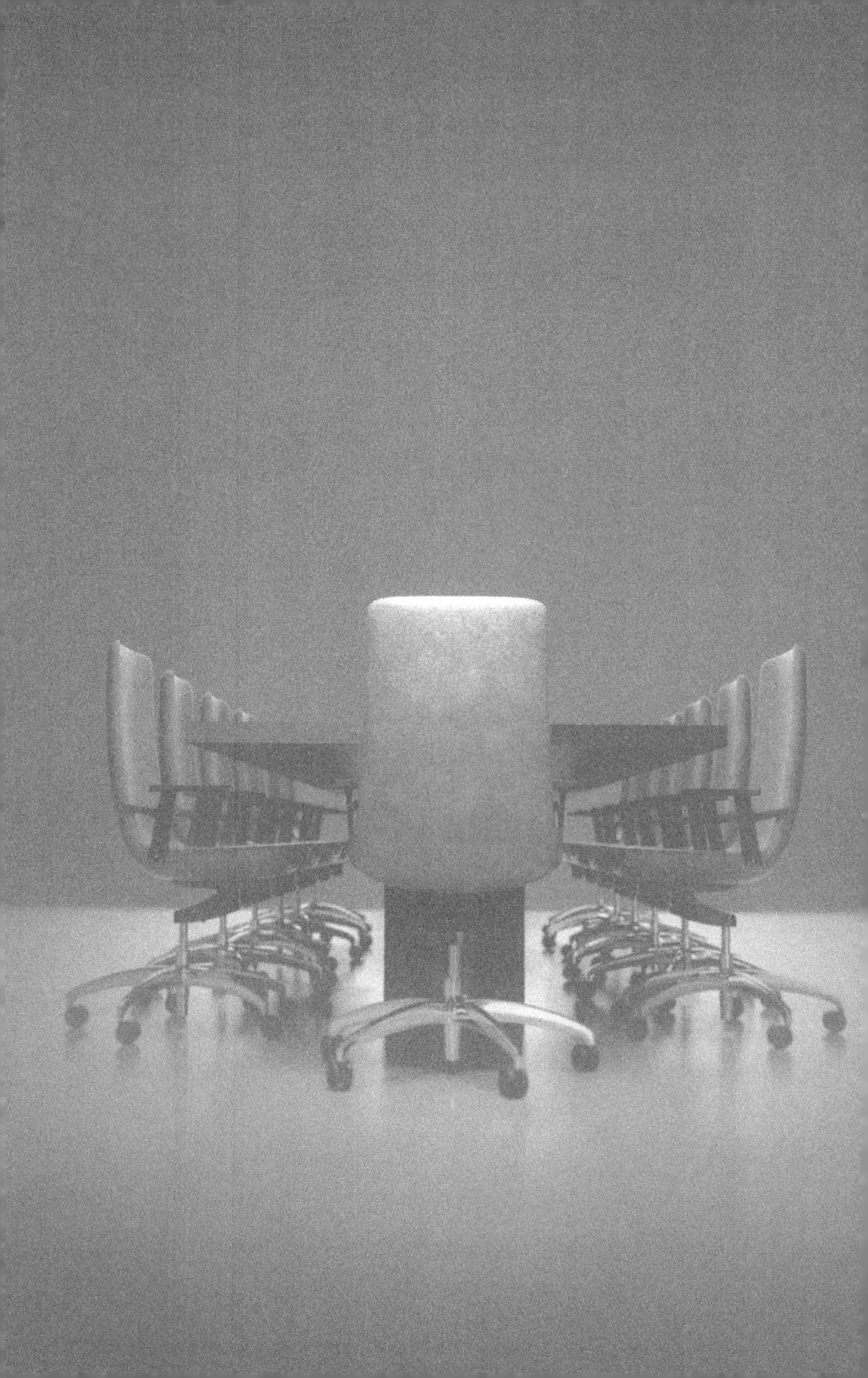

CHAPTER 4

Managing through Influence Is a Game Changer

I was recently interviewed by 4word, a Christian organization helping women to accelerate their careers, on the topic of becoming a woman of influence. I was surprised to find out that, before they asked me to lead this discussion, they had a difficult time finding a woman executive to agree to lead on this topic. Apparently, a lot of the women they approached—who were all very successful in their careers—didn't want to be seen as bragging. They shied away from seeing themselves as a woman of influence. And yet, influence is really about changing lives and outcomes: helping people to do more than they think they can do on their own.

Why wouldn't anyone want to identify as someone like that?

Lean In and McKinsey & Company's 2023 "Women in the Workplace" report[12] revealed that while women enjoy holding the power and the influence that comes with leadership roles, they often encounter more stress and scrutiny than their male counterparts. And

---

12 "Women in the workplace 2023," LeanIn.Org and McKinsey & Company, 2023, https://www.mckinsey.com/featured-insights/women-in-the-workplace.

that scrutiny and stress starts young. Research funded by the Dove Self-Esteem Fund revealed that "7 in 10 girls believe they are not good enough or do not measure up in some way, including their looks, performance in school and relationships with family and friends."[13] No wonder so many of us lack the confidence to see ourselves as leaders or pursue a leadership track.

Still, I believe there is another big reason women don't want to identify themselves as influential. They are confusing the concept of influence with *management.*

What Management Is ... and Isn't

According to *Merriam-Webster,*[14] *management* is defined as "the conduction or supervising of something, such as a business or organization." That's a pretty broad definition, open to a lot of interpretations. But for women, many of those interpretations fall on the negative side.

Another of my mentees—a really talented young woman in her early thirties—recently called me in a panic because she was being asked to consider a promotion to a sales manager role. I told her I thought that was amazing, because, well ... I did. Then I asked her, "What's the problem?"

"I don't want to be one of those people that just sits behind a desk all day and pushes paper around, calling my team nagging at them every day, micromanaging all of their activities throughout the day," she said.

---

13 "Statistics on Girls & Women's Self Esteem, Pressures & Leadership," Heart of Leadership, https://heartofleadership.org/statistics/.

14 *Merriam-Webster's Collegiate Dictionary,* s.v. "management" (n.), www.merriam-webster.com. https://www.merriam-webster.com/dictionary/management#:~:text=noun,something%20(such%20as%20a%20business).

I started laughing and told her, "It's great that that's *not* what you want to do, because that would make you the worst manager on the planet. That has nothing to do with what a great sales manager looks like."

My mentee was telling herself a story of what management looks like that simply is not true. Much of our narrative comes from our own experiences of being managed. Maybe you had a nightmare boss or a bad coach and swore, "I will never, ever, ever be *that* person." Maybe you simply think managing people sounds hard. And don't get me wrong—if you're responsible for people management, it's not always easy. Of course you need to ensure your employees are meeting expectations and doing their jobs and that you are "supervising" them. But great management is about so much more than telling people what to do. It's about *influence*. And through influence, you can have a huge impact in helping people and perhaps even change their lives. Just like any strong coach or teacher, you can inspire and perhaps even help your team to accomplish goals they had no idea they could do on their own.

That's how you win hearts and minds. And that's how you build that path to the C-suite.

Managing through Influence

Earlier, I mentioned that I was planning to quit my job and write a book at the age of thirty-five. Before I got around to turning in my resignation, I was called into a meeting with my boss's boss, Doug. This man was a very senior executive in the company, so it would have been understandable if I was a bit nervous. But I wasn't nervous. In my mind, I was leaving the company. What was the worst that could happen in this meeting? I mean, he could fire me. I went into this meeting with no agenda and immediately started to describe everything I thought was wrong with the company (and it was a long list). I told him that sales wasn't working with marketing, marketing wasn't working with operations, all these groups were not working together, and the company was going in the wrong direction from where we needed to go.

When I had finished my rant, Doug didn't hesitate. "Do you want to come work for me?" he asked.

That's why I didn't quit my job.

There has been a lot of talk recently about "quiet quitters," and I think it applies to many employees. They either stop trying, or they leave without giving their boss a chance, just as I was about to. But if you're really out the door, if you're really unhappy, you owe it to yourself and your company to be honest with your executive team. You're not going to get fired because you express that you're unhappy, unless you're really struggling in your job. In that case, if you dislike your job enough that it causes you to underperform, both you and your company will probably benefit from your departure.

If, on the other hand, you are doing a good job and are a person who has earned the respect of your manager and their peers, your supervisors will most likely appreciate your feedback on why you're frustrated, and your ideas to help the company succeed.

You could even wind up with a whole new job.

My new job was to solve not only the problems I ranted about but to solve other complex problems that required the entire company to come together. It wasn't the first time I'd played that kind of role. As an individual contributor or as a sales manager, if I saw a problem, I was always that person who would say, "Hey, this is broken. I bet if we got this person and that guy and this gal, we could make some progress here." But now it was my actual job, and it was a perfect role for me—because it presented an amazing opportunity to become a person of influence in my company.

Doug's vision at the time that I took on this new role was that we needed to build and invest in our channel partners to be a primary demand generation vehicle for the company, while also doing a better job of enabling our partners to sell our solutions on their own. Scaling through our partners was the answer to taking our organization to the next level, but building this new flywheel was not something we had done before inside our company. That was the problem statement. Everyone was doing their best—the sales teams were working hard, the marketing team was working hard, the channels team was on overdrive, everyone was doing everything they could think of to solve the problem—but we were solving a *new* problem for our company. And change management is difficult for any company, let alone a Fortune 100 company.

So, what did we do? With sponsorship from my boss, I went to the smartest, and yes, the most influential people inside the sales organization. I worked alongside the sales and channel VPs who were working around the clock to lead this change. I found those same smart, influential people in marketing, operations, and finance, calling them all together to say, "Hey, we have this problem, and I know we're all working on it, but what would happen if we were to all work on it together? What if we were to take the best and brightest ideas for each of our teams—at all levels—and build them into one unified strategy?"

And that is exactly what we did. Everyone came together to play their part. The result? We created one of the most powerful channel strategies in the industry. All these teams came together to solve a problem that they all very much wanted to solve independently, but we were so much more powerful together. And all this was done by influence. I want to be clear that this was a team effort; my role was simply to be the conductor. Not one of these groups *had* to work with me, not one of these teams reported to me, but they all had something to gain from solving the problem, and all realized the best way to succeed was to work together as one united team.

One thing I believe was important to our success was that we gave all the credit away. When you run a program or a project, regardless of what level you are, it's crucial to shine a spotlight on the people who make the project successful. I see managers and leaders make this mistake all the time—they use the "I" word. "I did this." "I did that." If you're a manager, everyone knows you are the manager. When you give all the credit away, when you lift up the people who came together to make it all happen, all the credit comes back to you indirectly. And the people who you held up, they'll want to work with you again and again.

After two years of working for Doug, who by this time had clearly become a strong mentor to me, I looked at him and said, "I can't believe what we've achieved in the last two years, and no one even reported to me. We accomplished all of this simply working cross-functionally with all of the other teams."

Doug didn't hesitate in his response. He said, "My advice for you is to spend the rest of your career pretending that no one reports to you. At the end of the day, they know you're the boss, but people do things for their reasons, not for yours. If you can win their hearts and minds and bring people together in a cohesive strategy, you'll be unstoppable."

That advice shaped my entire career.

Leading to Win

As I've said a few times, the easiest way to get a promotion is to start modeling what it takes while you're in the current job. That's why I think managing through influence is so important. The higher you go in the company, the more critical influence becomes, because you can't possibly touch all the employees in your organization. To be in the C-suite, your job is really to help make the company better, not just your own function. A CFO (chief financial officer) is not just thinking about the finance team—the CFO is thinking, *Does R&D have what they need to be successful? Is sales and marketing as efficient as they could and should be?* This should be true for every leader inside the C-suite. All these people have to be superior at managing through influence.

I've always tried to surround myself with the best people at different levels regardless of my role. I've always felt like I'm not the sharpest tool in the shed, but if I can surround myself with really sharp people and learn from them, that's just so much easier than trying to figure it all out on my own. And I always worked to give the credit away, as at the end of the day, it is my team who truly deserved all the credit. Now let's hear from a master of influence, Blair Christie.

TRANSFORMATIONAL LEADER: BLAIR CHRISTIE, FOUNDER, CEO, BOARD MEMBER, AND ADVISOR

Blair Christie is a seasoned executive with extensive experience in marketing, communications, and corporate strategy. She is currently the founder and chief executive officer (CEO) at Denim, a software company designed to revolutionize work for the frontline workforce, an independent board member who previously served as the senior vice president and chief marketing officer of Cisco Systems, where she led global marketing, government affairs, technology policy, and corporate communications. Blair has a stellar background leading large teams and driving growth through strategic initiatives. Her career is marked by a deep understanding of technology and its impact on business, which has allowed her to lead transformative marketing and communications campaigns across various sectors.

***

When it comes to influence, it's not the moment that counts—it's the moments before the moment you need someone that count the most. When I was leading investor relations for Cisco, every three months I was responsible for orchestrating our quarterly shareholder conference calls. I was responsible for pulling together an entire quarter's worth of information, bringing it together with a compelling message, and delivering it to Cisco's CEO ... who happened to have a photographic memory and could be counted on to catch even a tiny error! I needed people across the company to work with me as quickly as possible to represent the whole of their organization. I was representing them, so it was important they trusted me and believed I had their best interests in mind, so I became very, very deliberate in building relationships throughout the two and a half months ahead of this moment. I learned to invest in relationships for the moments when I would need people—helping them and bringing value whenever they needed it. Stepping up when they needed me most, knowing I would rely on them later. When I did, they were there for me, and often went above and beyond. I believe it was because I had been there for them.

If you're looking to grow your influence in your career, here is my advice:

1. **Agility matters.** *Early in my career, I saw success as a very specific, linear path. But it's not always about going straight up the ladder. You can find success—and influence—in many ways, including making other people successful and moving across organizations, not just up.*

2. **Be kind to yourself.** *Doubt yourself less by having more conversations outside your own head. Don't let your internal narrative bring you down. Make sure you bring others into your dialogue for their perspectives and insight so you get the clearest picture possible. Seek feedback and ask questions, even if you might not like the answers, and don't be afraid to seek input from your adversaries, as well as your supporters.*

3. **Get support.** *Finally, choose the right partner. When people ask me, "How do you do it?" my answer is always "It's 'how do we do it?'" My husband is a critical part of my journey. He is part of my story and my success—not just because he loves me and thinks I'm great—but because he is both supportive of my work and confident in his own, which allows me to fly!*

In the end, if the idea of leadership doesn't sound rewarding to you, most likely you're telling yourself a story about what a leadership role really is. Let go of the false narrative that leadership means "management," and replace it with the idea that leading people is really all about influence, and you will be unstoppable.

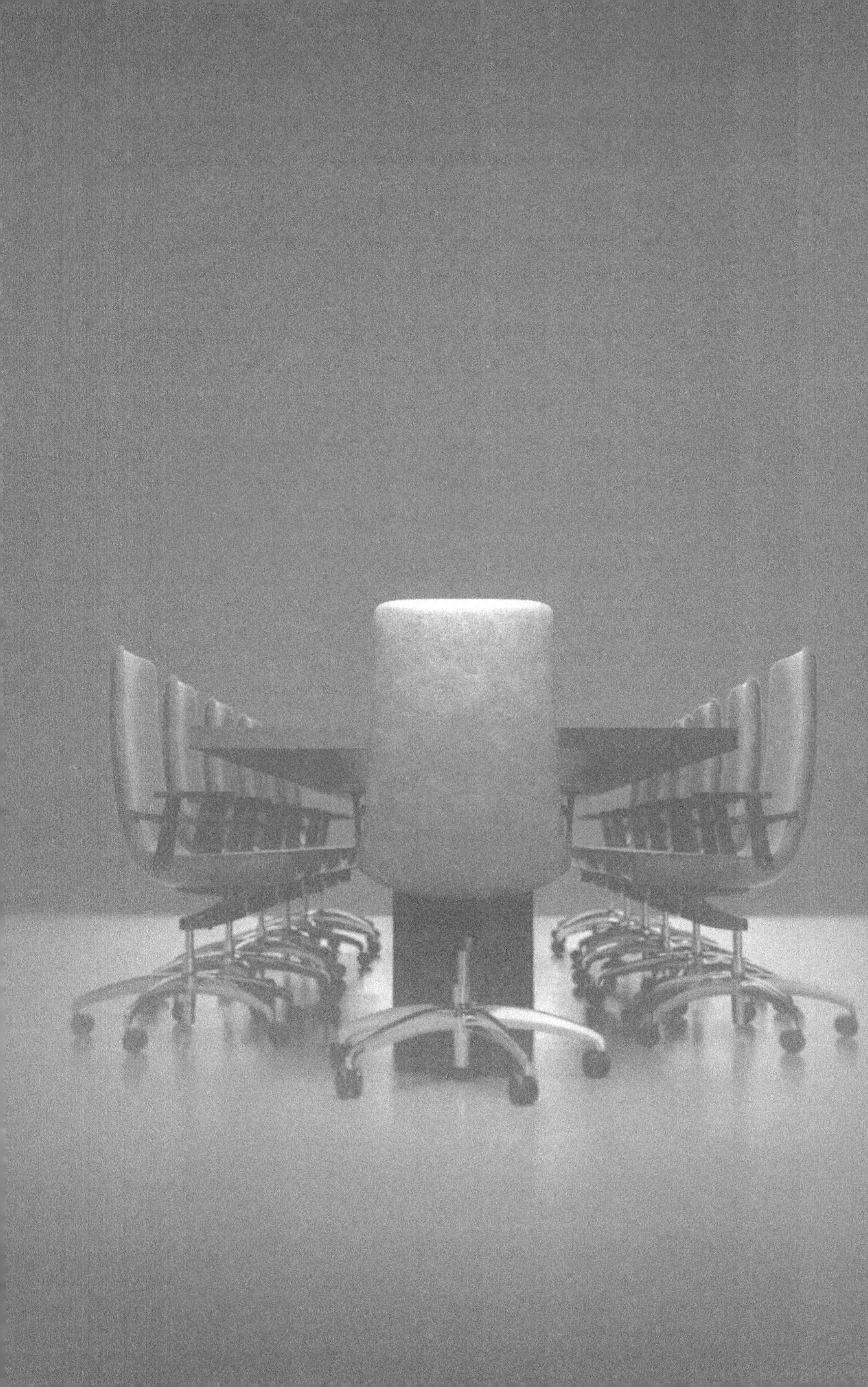

PART TWO

Break Away from the Pack

Now that we've built a foundation that will put you on a leadership track, it's time to start seeking out those experiences that will set you apart from your peers and establish you as a person capable of driving significant change to your organization's future. The following chapters will guide you through the process of distinguishing yourself as a rising star and a person to watch inside your organization. We will touch on how to find the right mentors at the right time, what to do when you think you've hit a ceiling in your current role, and when it is indeed time to move on, how to choose your next move carefully.

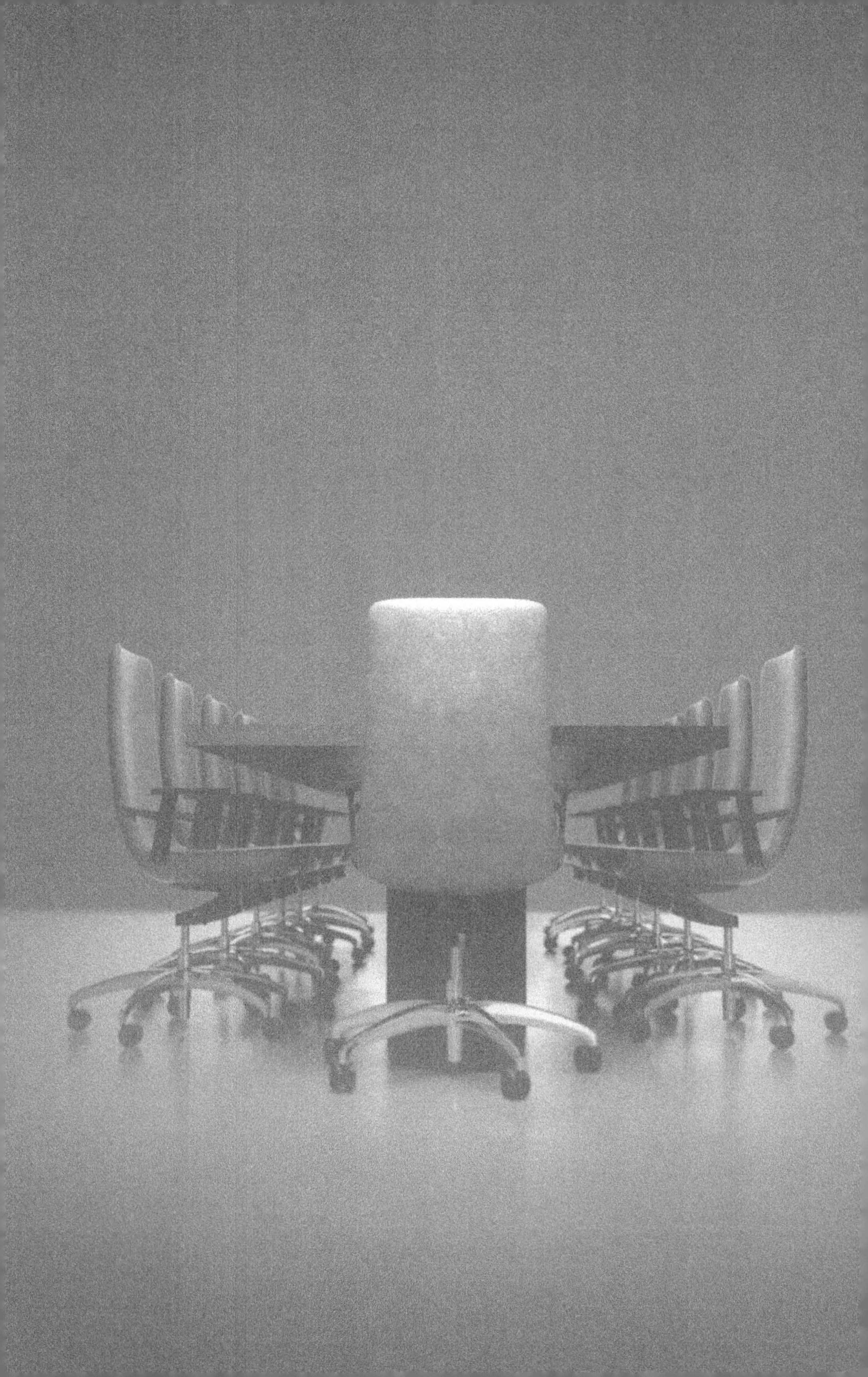

CHAPTER 5

Set a High Bar

I was twenty-five years old when I had the privilege of working for AT&T's number one sales manager in the US. I had just started with her team, and I was failing. She brought me into her office and told me, "We're going to create a little plan together."

My eyes welled up. I knew I was about to be fired.

She saw my reaction and took pity. "Okay, hold on a minute. Go outside my office and tell me what you see on the wall." I looked and saw a list of everyone on her team with their sales results, which of course were incredible. So, I took a deep breath, walked back into her office, and told her, "I saw that everyone on your team is over 150 percent of their sales goals."

She said, "Exactly. Now, what do you want to achieve?" I blurted out, "I want to get to 100 percent of my goal." (Secretly, I thought that was impossible. I was at 60 percent of my number and absolutely miserable.)

"I appreciate that," my manager replied, "but you can't be on my team if you want to be at 100 percent of your goal. You have to want to achieve something much, much bigger to be on my team. If you don't want to do something great, that is completely okay, but you can't be on my team. Think it over, come back tomorrow, and tell me what you want."

Now, I may be slow, but I am not stupid. I came in the next day, took a deep breath, and shared, "I want to be at 150 percent of my goal." She replied, "That's great. Now we're going to do the work."

She mapped out a plan with me; we worked very hard. We dove deep into the details of what it would take, and I finished that year at 180 percent of my goal. This manager changed my life, teaching me that we can only achieve what we set our sights on.

You Have to Believe It to Achieve It

There is no way around one fundamental fact: you can't get to the C-suite without being excellent at what you do. And I hope that by now we've established that I—a multi-C-suiter and multi-board member—am a regular human being. I've also explained that getting to the C-suite didn't just happen to me by magic. I worked for it. You can, too, and you can achieve incredible things.

But first, you have to *believe* you can. And if you're like a lot of women, underneath it all, you don't.

Recent research shows major differences in levels of self-confidence between men and women. In study after study, women underestimate their performance and capabilities compared to men, even when their actual performance is equal or better. In one study by the National Bureau of Economic Research (NBER), men and women took the same test and were asked to rate their performance. While their actual performance was basically the same, the men rated their performance at 61 out of 100, and the women rated theirs at 46.

This held true even when the participants were told that their self-assessments would influence hiring decisions.[15]

When it comes to getting hired, men are similarly bullish in their self-assessments. There's an urban legend about an internal Hewlett-Packard report that showed that men were applying for jobs when they met 60 percent of the qualifications, where women only applied to jobs when they met 100 percent of them. In reality, it appears to be a bit unclear as to whether there was an actual report—or perhaps this was an off-the-cuff comment by an HP exec. But women do consistently hold themselves to higher standards than men.[16] The question is *why?*

There's a great book called *The Confidence Code: The Science and Art of Self-Assurance—What Women Should Know*[17] by Katty Kay and Claire Shipman that digs into this issue. Basically, their thesis is that our collective lack of confidence is the result of a few factors, including the following:

- **Perfectionism.** We set high standards for ourselves and feel like we need to be perfect to be confident—which explains why we don't apply for jobs where we don't meet 100 percent of the qualifications.

- **Overthinking.** Women tend to ruminate more than men, which can lead to analysis paralysis that prevents us from taking risks and seizing opportunities.

---

15   Christine L. Exley and Judd B. Kessler, "The Gender Gap in Self-Promotion," National Bureau of Economic Research, May 2021, https://www.nber.org/papers/w26345.

16   Kaila Kea-Lewis, "Why 60% Qualified Is Enough, According to a Recruiter," *Inhersight*, July 6, 2021, https://www.inhersight.com/blog/insight-commentary/why-60-percent-qualified-is-enough.

17   Katty Kay and Claire Shipman, *The Confidence Code: The Science and Art of Self-Assuredness—What Women Should Know* (HarperCollins, 2014).

- **Failure and risk aversion.** In general, women aren't as comfortable with risk as men and fear failure more intensely than men. This can prevent us from stepping out of our comfort zones and taking on new challenges.

- **Biology.** Variations in hormones, brain structure, and chemistry might impact how men and women perceive risk and respond to stress.

- **Social conditioning.** As recently as 2023 according to McKinsey's aforementioned "Women in the Workplace" report, women in leadership still face backlash and negative stereotypes like being labeled as "bossy" or "aggressive."[18] *It actually said that. In 2023.*

- **Internalizing criticism.** Women are more likely than men to view negative feedback as proof of their inadequacies as opposed to an opportunity to learn and grow.

- **Lack of role models.** As you've seen, the pipeline is still not putting enough of us in these top positions.

- **Self-doubt.** As I mentioned earlier, women are more likely than men to experience impostor syndrome.

It all adds up to a toxic cocktail, and this book is not going to make all these things go away. But what this book can do is help you to develop a strategy to make aiming higher feel more natural, giving you a place to start and a template to follow to accomplish the big things that will build your confidence.

---

18 LeanIn.Org and McKinsey & Company, "Women in the Workplace 2024," McKinsey & Company, September 17, 2024, https://www.mckinsey.com/featured-insights/women-in-the-workplace.

CHAPTER 5

Find Your North Star

The first step is figuring out where you are best positioned to get something big done in your organization—something like what I described in the previous chapter, where you get a lot of people together to solve a problem that affects them all. So ... how do you figure out what that problem might be?

I used to love the TV show *Undercover Boss*. In one episode, a CEO for an airline puts on a disguise and a hard hat and starts lugging suitcases around alongside his frontline employees, while realizing just how impossible it is for them to do their jobs. I used to do a version of the same thing when I joined a company. Of course, I wanted to meet with the executives and senior managers, but in those early days I really wanted to meet the frontline folks in sales, in engineering, and in customer service who could tell me what was really going on. When I did, I asked them all kinds of questions. *If you were me, what are the three things you would change? What obstacles make your job impossible? What do our customers want us to do desperately and with urgency?*

If you really want to know the truth, people will tell you exactly what you need to do.

To me, that's how you develop strategy. It's how you find the North Star for your team or company. And it works at all levels. I don't care if you're a new manager or if you're a CEO; you can do it, and it's very powerful when you do. Figure out what the people who work with you and around you really want. What they need your help on to excel in their jobs. Something that will help your company as a whole (and of course something that will also look good on your résumé). Then focus on fixing it.

Call it the undercover boss strategy. (Unless CBS says we can't!)

59

Make a Plan

Once, when I was new in a company, I told my CEO that one of my "calls to action" for my organization was to have a plan to go big. His deadpan response to my enthusiasm was, "Can we just ask them to have a plan?"

I laughed. I thought he was joking, but he was completely serious. "Tracey," he told me, "most people don't have a plan. They're just winging it. They get up every morning, they work hard, but they don't have a plan. So can we just ask them to have a plan?"

It won't matter how big and bold your North Star is if you don't have a plan to get there. So, in honor of my former CEO and your future as a CEO, let's make a plan.

1. Get clear on your vision. Focus on that North Star and make sure it's big enough to make a difference.

2. Gather your dream team (the best of the best at *all* levels) together and agree on the three to five things you need to do to get to where you want to go. These will become your initiatives for the year.

3. Establish clear metrics and timelines as to what you're going to achieve and when. And make sure your dream team helps you set these metrics in order to buy into them!

4. Put your plan in writing (if it's not in writing, it's not a plan).

5. Communicate your plan before launching with your boss, their boss, other key cross-functional partners, and people close to the customer for feedback. You want them to be part of your plan. Take their feedback seriously and ask for their support so your plan becomes *their* plan.

6. Decide how you will celebrate wins and share credit with all who participate.

7. Communication is critical. Once launched, have a plan to consistently share your strategy with your organization. Be clear on your goals and how you will measure progress, and give credit to all those amazing people who helped you create this plan.

8. Test often what is working and what is not with people closest to the customer. Adjust as necessary and keep lifting up those who are driving change. This will inspire others to follow.

TRANSFORMATIONAL LEADER: SHEILA JORDAN, SENIOR VICE PRESIDENT, CHIEF DIGITAL TECHNOLOGY OFFICER

Sheila Jordan is Honeywell's senior vice president, chief digital technology officer, responsible for all digital transformation efforts across the company, broad oversight and responsibility for IT infrastructure, end user support, the more than one hundred services delivered through applications, and the expansion of software development to support Honeywell's digital initiatives and go-to-market offerings. Before Honeywell, Sheila was senior vice president and chief information officer at Symantec, served as senior vice president of communication and collaboration IT at Cisco Systems, and worked for Walt

Disney World, where she was the senior vice president of Destination Disney. She has received numerous awards and honors, including being inducted into the 2023 CIO Hall of Fame by CIO Magazine, inclusion in Forbes' 2023 CIO Next List, recognition among Technology Magazine's 2022 Top 100 Women in Technology, and a 2019 Women of Influence Award from the Silicon Valley Business Journal. She is also the author of *You are NOT Ruining Your Kids: A Positive Perspective on the Working Mom.*

***

In our family, we have a New Year's Eve tradition where we share a quiet dinner with extended family and friends, reflect on the year, and talk about our plans for the year ahead. I always used that time to think about the job that I wanted not that year, but three years down the line (because five is too long and one is too short).

At one point, I decided I wanted to be the CIO (chief information officer). Our CIO at the time was a fantastic leader, she and the CEO had a great relationship, so I knew I wasn't going to be seeing that C-suite anytime soon. Still, I knew what I wanted, so I took a SWAT inventory to get a sense of where I was doing well, as well as any weaknesses I still needed to overcome. This was a really important step for me. When you truly do the work to identify your weaknesses, you can then fill in the gaps so that no one can look at your résumé and say, "Well, you don't have this experience." Today, I have reached my goals and more.

If you're hoping to forge your own path to the C-suite, here are my suggestions:

1. **Own your career.** I *often tell people, especially early in their careers, "You own your career; don't give that up to your manager, don't give it up to your boss, don't give it up to a colleague."*

2. **Be planful, but available.** *There will be times when you will get tapped on the shoulder to do something that isn't in your plan. When you're tempted to say, "I'm not qualified," or, "I can't," resist it. Your leader sees the ability for you to do something different than what you're doing now. It's those moments when you feel uncomfortable, when you don't have all the answers, that you grow the most.*

3. **Ask for the promotion.** *There hasn't been a single promotion in my entire career that I didn't ask for. You can't be obnoxious about it, but it's perfectly okay to tell your boss that you'd like to get promoted and ask what you should be working on to get there. Make sure you're incorporating any feedback into your plan—the worst thing you can possibly do is ask for feedback and then ignore it.*

In our next chapter, we'll talk about the secrets of building a breakthrough team that will help power you and your dreams to the next level.

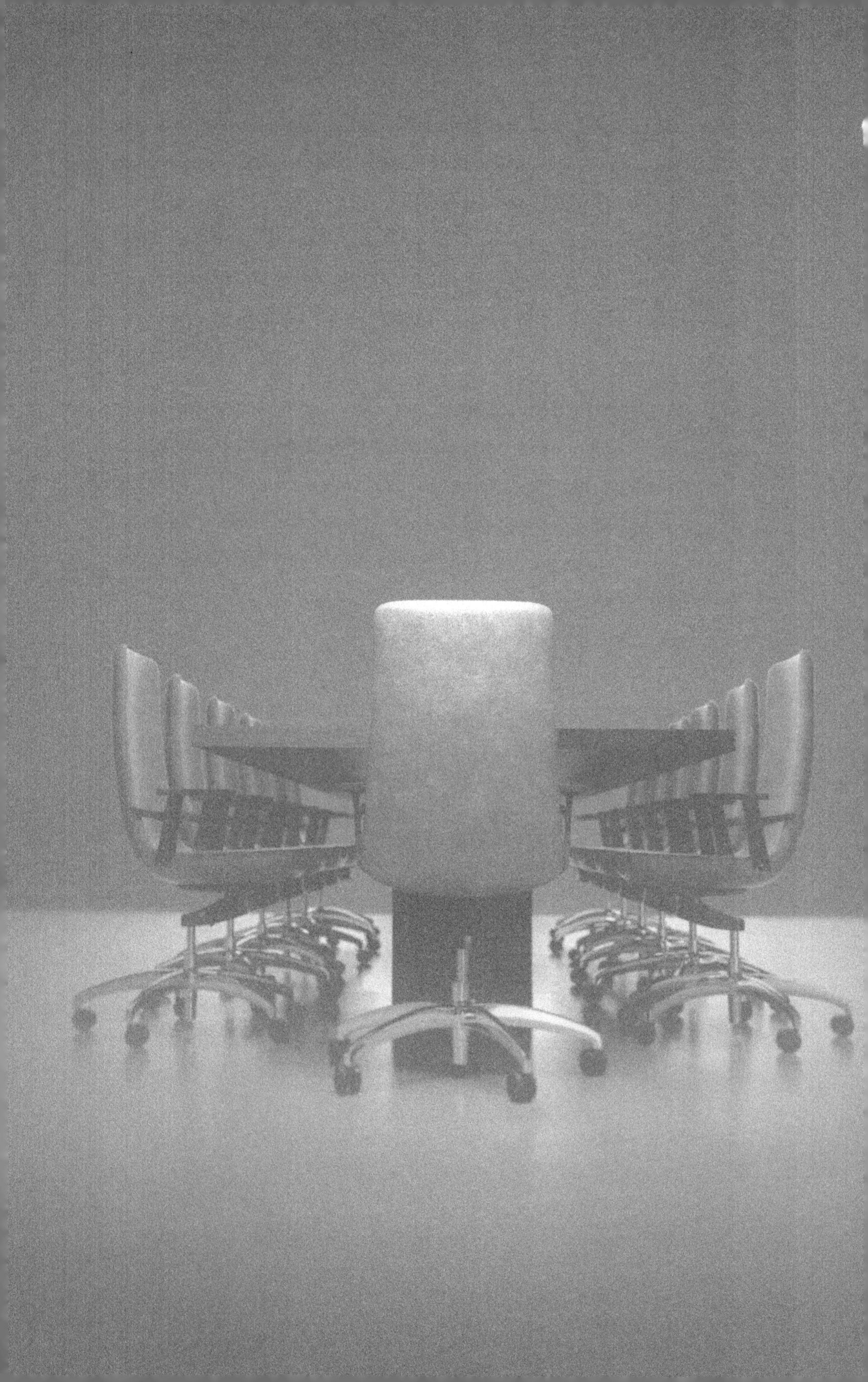

CHAPTER 6

Hire Your A-Team

I had just taken my first VP role running a $1 billion business. I knew I needed a business partner who was the best of the best, and I knew exactly who that person was. We had been peers at the same organization in different functional roles, and early on, I noticed that this person really stood out. He was extremely bright, polished, confident, and well known as someone who always did what he said he was going to do. He was the kind of person who, if you gave him a problem, would come back the next day with a bunch of ideas. He could easily be promoted for this job and also the next job. And people just *liked* him. He was my dream hire.

The only problem? He had been someone else's dream hire too. Which was why he had started a new position in our company only four months before.

I knew his current job had been a lateral move for him. The position I was offering was a big step up. So, I called him and told him, "Hey, I have a much bigger job for you. You're going to help me run a billion-dollar business."

He turned me down. He had given his new management team his word, and he felt like leaving after four months would be a bad move. He would be leaving them all in the lurch. How would that look?

I understood his concerns. But I was not willing to give up so easily. I replied, "I understand, but I want you to step back for a minute. I want you to think about what our CEO would want you to do. Would he rather have you stay in this role that you've been in for four months, which impacts a $300 million business, or would he rather you drive a billion dollars' worth of business for the company? Which is more impactful for our shareholders?"

He laughed and said, "Well, you raised a good point. Let me think about it."

He ended up accepting my offer, and we got along famously. From then on, wherever I went, he was always my first call. I circled back to him every time because he was a problem solver who was very good at strategy and execution, and as I said before, people really, really liked him. It's rare when you can find someone with all those attributes.

By the way, he's the CEO of a $1 billion-plus company today.

Hiring Matters

Hiring the right employees should result in one important metric: improved performance. While productivity can be measured in infinite ways, a great employee will always raise the bar inside your organization. How much impact? According to McKinsey, top talent is up to eight times more productive than the average.[19] That's why the saying that A-players hire A-players is true. If you get promoted to

---

[19] Scott Keller, "Attracting and Retaining the Right Talent," McKinsey & Company, November 24, 2017, https://www.mckinsey.com/capabilities/people-and-organizational-performance/our-insights/attracting-and-retaining-the-right-talent.

a level where you're managing people or managing managers, there's nothing more critical than your ability to bring the right people into your organization. You truly are only as good as your team, and to do great things, your team should consist of people who can not only do the job they've been hired to do but also the next job from there.

Hiring skills are a critical component of making it to the C-suite because the need to locate and reel in these A-players never really ends. There's never a right time to stop working on building your team, finding the best people, nurturing them and bringing out the best in them, setting the bar higher with each person you hire. A-players aren't easy to find, but they're out there in every function—and if you're the manager who is known for bringing them in, you get noticed.

The best way to make sure you end up with the right people is to have a formal process to help you identify them. I was lucky to start my people-managing career at AT&T, where the training was top notch. They taught us to ask experiential questions in interviews as opposed to hypothetical ones; instead of, "What would you do in X or Y situation?" focus on their actual experience. Start with, "Tell me about a time when you faced an impossible situation. How did you handle it, and what was the outcome?" That's the way I interview, and the way I encourage you and everyone on your interview panel to approach the process. My goal is to understand what the A-players do intuitively in my organization and then devise a series of questions that delve into a candidate's actual, real-life experiences to understand if they truly have what it takes to join my team.

Working with some of your "best people," put all those attributes down on paper before you start talking to candidates. Then develop your interview questions to screen for the specific attributes you're looking for, looking for individuals or leaders with a consistent track record of breakthrough results. Past experience is *always* the best predictor of how a new hire will perform in your organization.

Recruiting as a Strategic Partner

As you climb the ladder, you won't be able to participate in every interview—so how can you hang on to your power to influence how interviews are conducted? I always worked directly with my recruiting team. Whenever I joined a new company, even if I was the president, I'd always sit down with the recruiting team for one of my first meetings and ask them: "Who are our best people? Why are they so good? What companies did they come from? Who are the people who are struggling or even leaving our organization, and which companies did they come from? What common attributes do they share?" I would then ask the team to use those characteristics to create a template for the qualities we needed in new hires. I also worked directly with our recruiting team on our value proposition, sharing why our company was the most exciting company to join, to ensure we attracted the highest quality rock star candidates possible.

Lastly, I always empowered the recruiting team to call me directly if we were making a poor choice, sharing that our future depended on hiring only the best of the best. I promised to keep their name out of any actions on my part as a result of their concerns. And they called often to stop a mistaken hire from happening. Thank goodness!

Go for Grit ... Then Keep Going

One of the most essential attributes I ask recruiters and managers to look for is *grit*. I remember joining a new company, meeting some of the team and thinking, *I'm not sure if they're the right person for this role,* only to find, just a year later, I was completely wrong. What I missed in those early discussions was the fact that some of these individuals had endless reserves of grit. No matter what hit them, they would get back up, dust themselves off, and find a different way to approach whatever problem they were facing. That's what grit is—the ability to bounce back and stick with what is required no matter what it takes. It matters a lot. It can really define people.

University of Pennsylvania psychologist Angela Duckworth, who has studied what grit is and how it works, defines it as a combination of "resilience, hard work, and a sustained effort toward achieving long-term objectives. It involves both perseverance (the ability to persist in the face of setbacks) and passion (consistent interest over time)."[20] Duckworth's research has shown that individuals with higher levels of grit are more likely to achieve success across a wide range of different pursuits and professions, including (but not limited to) education, military training, and competitive sports. Grit predicted retention in the United States Military Academy at West Point as well as success in the National Spelling Bee, and it did it better than other, more obvious factors like IQ or physical fitness. In studies that tracked individuals over time, Duckworth's results also suggested that "gritty" people are more likely to attain higher levels of education and career success.

Sports can be a great measure of whether or not a person has grit, especially if they played for a long time and were successful. I feel the same way about anything that forces people to be competitive while also working as a team. These individuals deal with loss and disappointment regularly and keep pushing forward; they are accountable

---

20 A. L. Duckworth, C. Peterson, M. D. Matthews, and D. R. Kelly, "Grit: Perseverance and Passion for Long-Term Goals," *Journal of Personality and Social Psychology*, 2007.

for their actions and make adjustments and corrections in order to achieve their goals.

In addition to grit, there are several other attributes I consider essential when I'm hiring:

- **Breakthrough results.** I look for problem solvers with a proven track record of setting lofty goals, and a history of getting big things done for their organization.

- **Agility.** Business is always changing, and whoever I hire needs to be able to pivot when necessary, without losing their cool.

- **Staying power.** Some people believe that switching jobs every two years is necessary for career growth. I believe that job hopping and changing companies every eighteen to twenty-four months can be a big mistake. It is very difficult to show proven results if you're moving from company to company every eighteen months, so I look for people who have proven staying power—that means three to five years. But do be careful with new hires who have been with the same company for twenty years. There are, of course, exceptions, but ensure you assess in detail their ability to adapt well to a new role and a new company.

- **Consistent promotions.** Hire people who can demonstrate a pattern of consistent learning and growth during their time with their previous employers. A track record of consistent promotions indicates they will likely continue to grow with you.

- **Complementary skills.** A great hire is someone who fills in your gaps. I always think of one of my leaders who would introduce himself to the group by saying, "I like to do all of the things Tracey hates." While it made everyone laugh (including me), I always did try to hire people who had different skills than me, as diversity brings strength to all teams. As I mentioned earlier, I also like people who will argue with me. I used to tell my team, "I try to be right more than I'm wrong, but I do get it wrong sometimes. And your job is to tell me when I'm wrong." Giving people permission to challenge me by creating a safe environment to do so was critical to my success. We always ended with a better result. (Of course, I'd always prefer constructive criticism, but the key message was if there's a problem, I want to know about it.)

- **Emotional Intelligence.** High IQ is great, but high *EQ* is critical too. Does your prospective hire understand how to relate to people, and do people want to be with them?

- **Energy giver.** Some people are energy takers who suck the life out of the room. Others seem to light up whatever group they're in. I used to say, "If I wouldn't go out to dinner with the person, then how could we expect a customer to go out to dinner with them?" Obviously, we all click with different people for different reasons, but I generally look for collaborators with good, positive energy that others will want to work with.

- **Sense of humor.** My father once told me, "If you have a sense of humor, you'll go far in this world; and if you don't, life can be hard." I like to have fun at work, so I try to hire people who make work fun and enjoyable, keeping morale high, especially when faced with difficult situations.

(For the record, I am cautious of prima donnas. Folks who think they're the smartest person in the room, don't play well with others,

or break a great deal of glass inside the organization typically don't do well for a long period of time inside any company.)

Keep in mind that these are *my* desired attributes; your own "must-haves" may be similar, and they may be different. What matters most is that you take some time to think through what qualities matter more to you and define them in writing ahead of time for anyone interviewing your new-hire candidates so all are clear on exactly what (and who) you're looking for to ensure you hit a home run with this new hire.

Diversity Matters

One final factor that's essential to consider in your hiring strategy is diversity. The term diversity, equity, and inclusion (DEI) has become a hot topic in some circles recently, but the underlying fact remains indisputable: *Diversity is good for business.* The more diversity you have in the room in terms of race, gender, age, sexual orientation, ability—you name it—the stronger your organization is going to be. Why? Because at the end of the day, people work with companies that represent them. The more diversity you have within your organization, the wider range of customers you're going to be able to attract, and the more differentiated your company will become.

It makes sense logically, but there's also a ton of research that backs this up. Here are just a few statistics from the current year, 2024:

- According to McKinsey, companies in the top quartile for gender diversity on executive teams were 25 percent more likely to have above-average profitability than companies in the fourth quartile. Companies in the top quartile for ethnic diversity were 36 percent more likely to outperform on profitability.[21]

- The Boston Consulting Group (BCG) found that companies with more diverse management teams have 19 percent higher revenue due to innovation.[22]

- According to Deloitte, diverse companies enjoy 2.3 times higher cash flow[23] per employee and Gartner found that inclusive teams improve team performance by up to 30 percent in high-diversity environments. Yet only 40 percent of employees agree[24] that their manager fosters an inclusive environment.[25]

So, the bigger question is, "How do you achieve better diversity in your workplace?" Hiring for diversity can be a challenge for many complex reasons, but if you make it a priority, you can move the needle.

How to get started? As you begin to look for future hires, do it with diversity in mind. I am a believer in that you always want (and need) to hire the best candidate. But if there are no high-quality, diverse candidates in the interview process, how in the world are you

---

[21] Sundiatu Dixon-Fyle, Kevin Dolan, Vivian Hunt, and Sara Prince, "Diversity Wins: How Inclusion Matters," McKinsey & Company, May 19, 2020, https://www.mckinsey.com/featured-insights/diversity-and-inclusion/diversity-wins-how-inclusion-matters.

[22] "It's Time to Highlight the Business Opportunity of DEI Initiatives," BCG, March 5, 2024, https://www.bcg.com/publications/2024/highlighting-the-business-opportunity-of-dei-initiatives.

[23] Josh Bersin, "Why Diversity and Inclusion Has Become a Business Priority," joshbersin.com, December 7, 2015, https://joshbersin.com/2015/12/why-diversity-and-inclusion-will-be-a-top-priority-for-2016/.

[24] Josh Kostoulas, Melanie Lougee, and Jason Cerrato, "How HCM Technologies Can Scale Inclusion in the Workplace," gartner.com, January 22, 2020, https://www.gartner.com/en/documents/3979855.

[25] Kellie Wong, "Diversity and Inclusion in the Workplace: Benefits and Challenges," Achievers.com, March 25, 2024, https://www.achievers.com/blog/diversity-and-inclusion/.

going to increase diversity within your company? A best practice is to be sure you have qualified, diverse candidates in every hiring process, and if you don't, you don't start the interviews until you do. It's not easy, but if you force yourself to look outside your comfort zone and stick with it, you can and will make serious progress.

Hiring for Your Company's Future ... and Yours

As you're building your team, you need to hire the very best person you can find for the job, whoever that might be. I've seen instances where a leader was intimidated to hire someone who was older or more experienced than they were onto their team. I see that as a mistake. Bringing in the best people you can find shows confidence. My goal was to hire people who were smarter than me, who would push not only me but my entire team to do better.

As I shared earlier, one of my rules for hiring is to hire someone who can do the job I'm trying to fill, but who I believe can also do the next job—because people who aspire to do the next job will work harder. They will do whatever it takes to crush it in the role that you're hiring for because they know that to move to the next level, they're going to have to go above and beyond. If you're hiring people who can do at least one or two jobs more than you're hiring for, you're going to have an amazing team.

Another rule is to be sure you always have somebody on your team who can be your backfill. Keep your team staffed with people who are ready and willing to do your job, and it will be that much easier for your leaders to say yes when it's time for you to move up to the next level. Let's hear from an expert, Luanne Tierney, on her hiring strategies to build your A-team.

CHAPTER 6

TRANSFORMATION LEADER: LUANNE TIERNEY, CMO AND BOARD MEMBER

Luanne Tierney is the go-to-market expert for companies looking to kick their marketing strategies into high gear. A sought-after public speaker, she is recognized globally for her insights and abilities to spot marketing trends. Luanne has honed her marketing skills over the past twenty-five years at some of the world's most important tech companies, including Apple, HP, and Cisco Systems. Luanne is a UC Berkeley graduate, passionate about developing career strategies for the next generation of leaders.

I once had a phone interview with a potential hire from a different industry. She was in the medical field and had no experience in tech. Our conversation flowed, revealing her quick thinking and adaptability. Intrigued, I decided to meet her in person.

During our face-to-face, I asked her, "What tools do you use? How do you approach complex problems?" Her answers impressed me so much that her lack of tech experience became irrelevant. I realized then that transferable skills, a willingness to be coached, and the courage to embrace new challenges are far more valuable than industry-specific knowledge.

I took a chance and hired her. Not only did she meet expectations, but she consistently exceeded them. I've since brought her to two other companies, and today, this young woman who started in the medical field is spearheading our AI initiatives across my entire marketing organization. I've found that people like that, who bring their creativity, ideas, and strong work ethic forward without hesitation, are the ones who drive the company forward.

If you're aiming to build a top-notch team, here are my tried-and-true suggestions:

1. **Hiring is a Relationship:** *While I'm an advocate for distributed teams, there's undeniable value in face-to-face interactions. Whether grabbing coffee or taking a walk, these personal moments reveal character traits that no resume can capture. I'm reminded of the legendary basketball coach, Coach K, who would invite potential recruits to dinner with his family. He paid close attention to how they treated his mother, a commercial house cleaner. This approach revealed their true nature—their respect, empathy, and social awareness. These qualities are essential for team dynamics but often remain hidden in formal interviews.*

2. **Look Beyond Degrees and Grades:** *In my experience, academic performance doesn't always predict career success. When hiring, I look for evidence of traits like creativity, adaptability, and real-world problem-solving skills. How have they overcome challenges? What creative solutions have they devised? I value seeing a track record of courage in taking on new responsibilities, consistent follow-through on commitments, and strong program management skills. These soft skills are potential indicators, far more than any degree or grade point average.*

3. **Create a Comfortable Environment for Candidates:** *We were interviewing for an inside sales position, and there was one candidate everyone loved—except me. Instead of dismissing her, I decided to have another conversation. I said, "Everyone thinks you're great, but I felt we didn't connect. Can you help me understand why?" Her honest response changed everything: "I was so*

nervous meeting you." This moment of vulnerability explained the disconnect and opened the door for a genuine conversation. I asked about her background, her aspirations, and even the books she was reading. Her true personality shone through as she relaxed—confident, insightful, and passionate. We hired her, and she's been promoted, doing fantastic work.

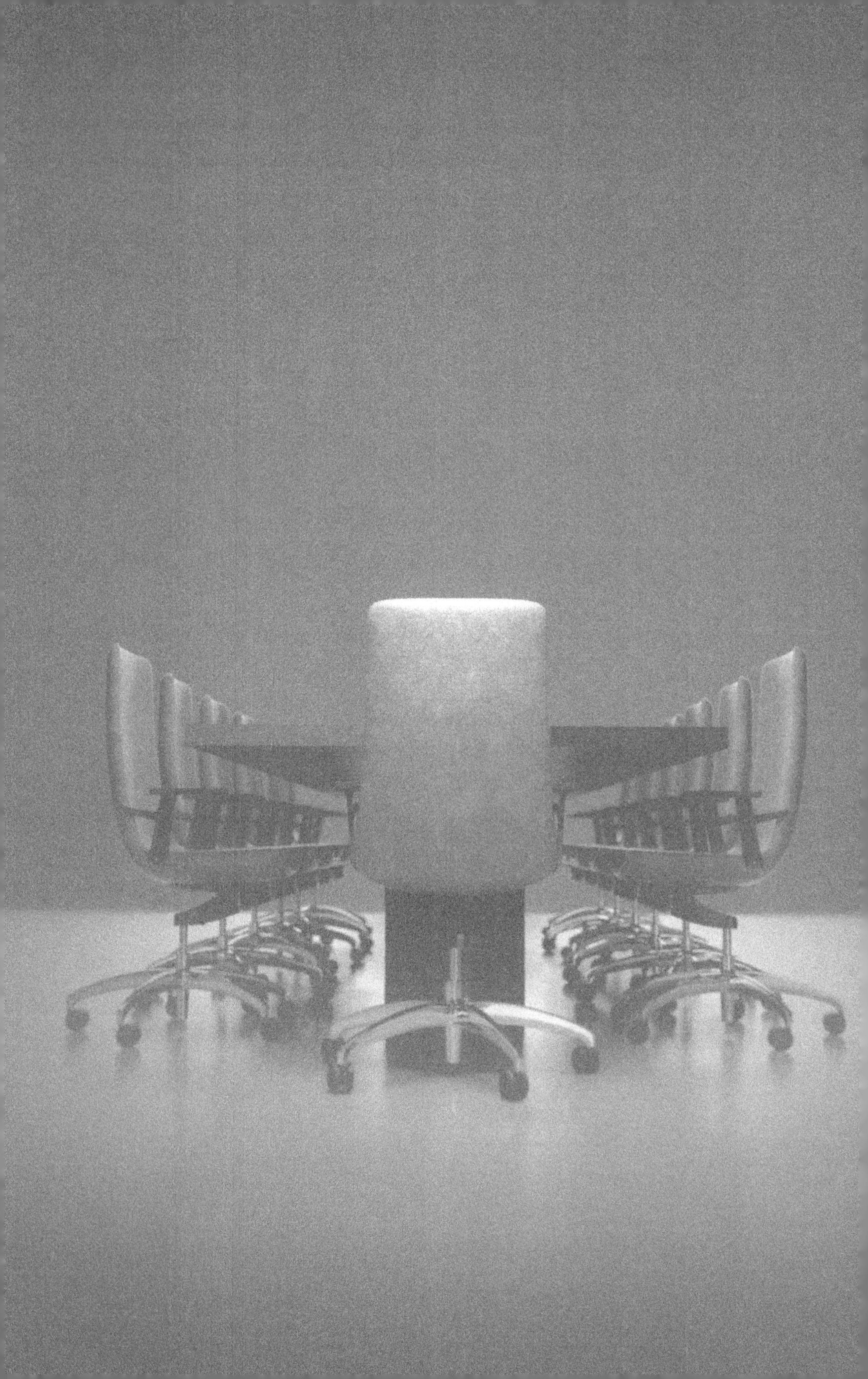

CHAPTER 7

The Founder's Mindset

I've already talked a little bit about my experience working for Cisco's public sector business—the job I was looking to leave when I was first planning to write this book. What I haven't talked about is what led up to that point ... which was actually what I consider to be one of my biggest successes.

When I was first promoted to manage Cisco's public sector team in the West, I was a manager with approximately a hundred people in my organization, and my new team's morale was at the lowest of lows. This was some time ago, and from the team's perspective, they needed help dealing with the complexity required to support these large, complex government customers. To add to the problem statement, the state of California was facing one of the largest deficits they'd seen in years. The governor of California had been impeached, and in the aftermath, any purchase over $50,000 needed sign-off by the state's chief information officer (CIO). And I was in charge of a business worth hundreds of millions of dollars whose primary client was the State of California.

So, what did we do? Well, for a bit, we felt pretty unlucky. We had what felt like one of the toughest jobs imaginable. I was not having fun … and it was probably not a lot of fun for those around me either.

And then, I decided to change gears.

I gathered the smartest people I could find to build our strategy together from the bottom up. As in a symphony, everyone had a different part to play, but all with the same end goal in mind. Everyone knew exactly what they needed to do to win. And we did. We took more market share that year than any competitor because we ran the same play together.

What was interesting was that initially, as I shared, when I came to the public sector team, the team felt that the company was not as focused on their success as was required. But within two to three years, all my private sector peers—the ones selling to Walmart and the many large accounts in the enterprise—were complaining in our leadership meetings: "Everybody wants to work on public sector. That's all anyone inside of the company cares about." It wasn't because we'd done anything brilliant. We had just cross-functionally come together, understood the big issues that we needed to resolve for customers and our shareholders, and executed like crazy. And we celebrated the milestones along the way. We approached the problem with a founder's mindset.

That's what this chapter is all about.

Thinking Outside Your Role

Every company has challenges. Every marketing, engineering, finance, or sales team has two or maybe two hundred things they could be doing better. The best leaders recognize the challenges that are keeping their CEOs and CFOs up at night and then bring people together cross-functionally to solve these problems. Personally, I've seen many of my promotions happen in the toughest economies, because those were pivotal moments when I had to adapt: to rethink, replan, and analyze how to use a difficult macro environment to help my company, employees, and customers emerge better and stronger. That's really where I was able to differentiate—because I love to approach problems the way a founder would.

I have the utmost respect for founders, as I have worked with—and *for*—some exceptional ones. These leaders started without employees, products, customers, and revenue, and they then had to convince investors to invest in their vision so that they could create their company. They're amazingly agile, because they have to be ready to pivot at a moment's notice. They don't see roadblocks; they simply see obstacles that they will need to go around. And they certainly aren't coming to a stop. They are masters at innovating and problem solving.

I used to tell my teams, "I don't expect any of you to start a company, but I do expect you to solve problems like a founder or CEO does." Whether you're an individual contributor or vice president, I'm looking for people who see a roadblock or problem and say, "Hey, this is driving me crazy, and it's a problem for the company. Let's build a team and go solve this. Let's knock this issue out of the way."

So, what does it really mean to lead like a founder? What should you be doing now that will demonstrate that level of problem-solving prowess we spoke about earlier in this book? The *Forbes* article "The Top Five Traits of Successful Startup Founders" offers a few clues. It outlines what it says are the five key characteristics that distinguish successful startup founders from those who don't make it:

PASSION

Successful founders are deeply passionate about their business. Passion is the secret sauce that means they never give up, that drives them to overcome obstacles and stay committed to their vision, even in the face of challenges.

VISIONARY THINKING

The founders who succeed are the ones with a clear and compelling vision who can anticipate market needs and innovate accordingly. They see opportunities where others might not and work toward capitalizing on these opportunities.

EFFECTIVE COMMUNICATION

Founders need to get other people on board to make their vision a reality, so they need to be able to articulate it to their team, investors, and customers in a way that gets them passionate about it as well.

TIME MANAGEMENT AND PRIORITIZATION

Founders need to get other people on board to make their vision a reality, so they need to be able to articulate it to their team, investors, and customers in a way that gets them passionate about it as well.

RESILIENCE AND RISK MANAGEMENT

No one hits a home run their first time at the plate, and founders know and accept this. They know failure is an unavoidable part of creating anything new, so they don't fear getting it wrong. Instead, they use the setbacks they face as learning opportunities to improve and adapt their strategies accordingly.[23]

These five traits allow founders to navigate the complexities of starting and growing a business and boost their odds of success. And they aren't traits that are exclusive to entrepreneurs. They're traits that anyone can cultivate and develop and grow—including you. It's really a matter of mindset, the core of that mindset being not seeing setbacks as obstacles but as objects you can learn to find your way around. It's about embracing the issues that most people see as difficulties as growth opportunities to find a new, better way forward. Doing this takes a little creativity, but more than that, it takes resilience.

Resilience is a critical component of the founder's mindset—it's the thing that enables you to navigate through challenges, adapt to changing environments, and keep going when everything around you seems to be collapsing. The COVID-19 pandemic was a critical test of business leaders' resilience, a phenomenon *Forbes India* examined in the article "Meeting the Spread of Coronavirus with a Contagious Resilience."[27] It included case studies of several companies who were able to adapt and pivot successfully. Some changed the way they operated, like supermarkets that added pickup and delivery services, while stores like Whole Foods and Target introduced special shopping hours for vulnerable customers. Others took on supply chain issues, like the IPO company BrewDog pivoting from making alcoholic beverages to producing hand sanitizers in the face of a shortage. This ability to come together, to pivot in the moment and to face big challenges, didn't just help the companies that weathered this one

---

26 Matt Carbonara, "The Top Five Traits of Successful Startup Founders," *Forbes*, May 13, 2021, https://www.forbes.com/sites/forbesfinancecouncil/2021/05/13/the-top-five-traits-of-successful-startup-founders/.

27 Patrick Reinmoller, "Meeting the Spread of Coronavirus with a Contagious Resilience," *Forbes India*, May 1, 2020, https://www.forbesindia.com/article/imd-business-school/meeting-the-spread-of-coronavirus-with-a-contagious-resilience/59119/1.

moment of crisis. Resilient companies frequently flex those muscles, so they are better able to deal with future changes and maintain a competitive edge.

And in the end, what are resilient companies made up of but resilient, smart people looking to drive change to help their companies succeed?

The founder's mindset is holding on to the belief that nothing is impossible, that what needs to happen will happen, because one way or another, you will make it happen. That may mean reaching out to talented people across different departments who can join you in moving the needle forward on a critical issue and helping you to get it done.

And make sure you always screen for a founder's mindset when you are hiring your A-team. Be clear about communicating your expectations and making it part of your culture. Most people come to their manager and say, "Hey, this difficult thing happened. What do I do?" To encourage a founder's mindset, the answer to that question should be, "What do you think *you* should do?" It's the idea of teaching people to fish as opposed to doing it for them.

TRANSFORMATIONAL LEADER: MARGARET FRANCIS, FORMER FOUNDER, SVP AT SALESFORCE

Margaret Francis is an SVP in the Office of the CEO at Salesforce. Previously she was an executive in residence at Costanoa Ventures, working in data, dev tools, ML/AI, cybersecurity and enterprise apps. The former CPO (chief product officer) of venture-backed dbt Labs, she has held various product and business leadership roles including president and COO of Armory (purchased by Harness); SVP of Salesforce Data Platform; and GM and SVP of Heroku. Prior to Salesforce, she was VP of product at Exact Target through its IPO, VP of product at Lithium, and co-founded two venture backed startups. She has also served as an independent board director for Sumo Logic.

I paid my way through art school writing code and doing technical work in the early days of the internet. When I got my MFA, I realized I would never earn enough to support a family, so I went to work for a digital agency and ultimately ended up working with many digital agencies. This gave me access to the boardroom very early in my career. I was in my twenties advising C-level executives on "what to do about the internet." I learned you bring a great deal of value when you know your stuff, even among people who seem much older and more experienced than you.

When I was about thirty, I started the first of two tech companies with a female co-founder—we had five kids under six between us, including tiny babies, so we had to balance a lot of what needed to be done between us. One of us would say, "I will be out having a baby—go run the board meeting." And the other would reply, "I will be attending a board meeting—deal with these customers." Some founders need to control everything, but we were physically and mentally incapable of that—so getting good at sharing what we could and could not do with very clear communication was really important. Beyond that, my best advice, whether you hope to become a founder or just think like one, is as follows:

1. **Communicate like you're in couples' counseling.** *Founders can be difficult. They knock down obstacles, they get stuff done, and they don't understand why the people around them can't. The reason is usually that they have information that you don't.*

> *You have to say, "Help me to understand what's going on…why this is so important…so we can share the same data and then operate our specific parts of this initiative."*

2. **Think of your career as many things you're going to do over fifty years…** *My second baby was born early and developed some problems, and I realized I had to leave my job at the company I had cofounded. It was the only time I quit a job that I really wanted, because my family was too important. I took a different job that gave me a little more of the structure and support I needed, and it ended up making me more money than I've made in any other job, save one.*

3. **…but do not stop working altogether.** *Trying to get back in after time out of the workforce is much harder than figuring out if there's a lateral step you can take, or a new capability you can develop, or a change you can make. Do not assume your partner is going to support you. It's a fatal mistake that women make professionally.*

The thing that separates successful founders from the rest of us is the ability to move past obstacles. Be a problem solver, not someone who simply points out the problem, communicate to your team that you expect them to stay focused on solutions, and you and your company will accomplish great things. In our next chapter, we'll take a closer look at another group of people who can help you do great things when we explore why mentorship matters and how to find the right one(s) for you.

CHAPTER 8

The Power of Mentorship

Earlier, I told the story of how, when I was about to quit my job, I went into a meeting with my boss's boss, vented my rather extensive frustrations with the company, and wound up leaving with a job offer. This executive, Doug, offered me a position as his sales strategy and operations leader. He said that he would have me shadow him in important meetings for six months, and then at the end of that period, I would know enough that I could be his right-hand person. Although the role didn't exist anywhere else in the company, I felt as though I didn't have anything to lose, and I accepted his very kind offer.

It turned out to be a life-changing move.

My new boss quickly became the most important mentor I had ever had. He followed through on his commitment to teach me much of what he knew. As a result, I learned more in six months than I had in the last ten years. We accomplished a great deal in those eighteen months and it never would have happened had Doug not seen something in me, and had he not encouraged me to do more.

Everyone needs these people in their life, to pull us aside and tell us we can do more than we might imagine, and then to take the time to help teach us how to move forward. So, in this chapter, we're going to look at how to find, reach out to, and maintain relationships with the right mentors.

Great Leaders Start with Great Mentors

Most people don't achieve greatness on their own. That's why so many companies offer formal mentorship programs within their organizations that are crucial to executive development. Eighty-four percent of CEOs who participated in formal mentoring programs reported that their mentors helped them avoid costly mistakes and become proficient in their roles more quickly. Additionally, 69 percent of these CEOs stated that mentoring relationships improved their decision-making abilities.[28] This type of formal mentoring is undoubtably important, but that's not what this chapter is about. This chapter is focused on *informal mentoring*, the kind of mentoring that occurs outside the structured programs provided by organizations, because *everyone* can create their own mentoring program.

Informal mentors can provide a lot of things a formalized, structured program cannot. When you choose your own mentors, you're more likely to receive advice that is relevant to your unique circumstances and career goals. The flexibility of an informal relationship means both mentors and mentees can engage in whatever way best fits their needs and schedules. Since these relationships develop organically based on mutual respect and shared interests, they allow a level of authenticity that can lead to deeper trust and more open commu-

---

[28] "Why Mentoring: What the Stats Say," McCarthy Mentoring, May, 2017, https://mccarthymentoring.com/why-mentoring-what-the-stats-say/.

nication between mentor and mentee than you'd probably find in a corporate program. And these relationships are crucial.

In other words, you need a mentor (or more likely, several mentors) to provide crucial advice and guidance on your journey to the C-suite. So ... *how do you find one?*

Finding Your Mentors

Finding a mentor doesn't have to be intimidating; all you really need is thirty minutes of someone's time once a month or even once a quarter. Start by identifying someone who is one or two levels above your current role and whose leadership style you admire. Ideally, this should be a person who is not in your reporting line, so they will not have a stake in your outcomes. Your mentor should be free to give you honest, unbiased advice.

Pull this person aside by email, text, or live conversation and simply say, "I really respect you. I am so amazed at what you've been able to achieve. Could I buy you a cup of coffee? Would you be up for meeting for thirty minutes in a month or so?" So far in my career I haven't met many people who will say, "No, I won't give you thirty minutes of my time," no matter how important or busy they are.

One thing you might *not* want to do is to start the conversation by asking someone, "Will you be my mentor?" It not only sounds too formal, potentially with someone you don't know well, but more importantly, it also sounds like you're asking for a great deal of time. And it doesn't need to be like either one of these things. To me, a good mentor-mentee relationship should happen naturally, based upon mutual respect and common interests.

Once you've set your first meeting with a potential mentor, take time to prepare. I can't tell you how many mentees showed up in my office and gazed at me like they were sitting at the feet of the yogi, waiting for me to magically impart nuggets of wisdom. When that happened, I would usually reply, "This is your meeting; what would you like to talk about? What's your agenda? What are you working on; where do you need help?"

Before you walk into that first meeting, get clear on your aspirations, what specific challenges you're facing, and what kind of guidance you are seeking. Do some digging into your mentor's background, experiences, and achievements, which will help you ask informed "How did you do this, handle that?" questions, similar to the experiential questions you should be asking during a job interview. Then draft a brief agenda outlining the key points you want to discuss.

And of course, be punctual and professional during the meeting. First impressions matter, so you want to kick things off by thanking your mentor for their time and willingness to help, sharing how much you value the opportunity to learn from them. (I always say that flattery will get you everywhere!) Ask thoughtful questions about their career journey, key decisions they made, and challenges they have faced.

When you have subsequent meetings with your mentor, don't assume they're going to remember what you talked about or the advice they gave you. That's your job. In your next meeting, remind your mentor, "We met last quarter, and this is what we talked about, and these are the three things that I have done as a result. It was really helpful, so thank you. What I'm thinking about next is this; can I get your feedback?" Or, "I'm trying to solve this problem that I'm currently facing." It's your time, so it's your job to manage and own that time.

Typically, at the end of the meeting, you will close with something like, "Thank you, this has been really helpful." You reiterate whatever action items you decided on, and, if you want to continue the relationship, you ask for a follow-up meeting within the next month, or three months, or whatever the appropriate timeframe is. Then you send an email confirming the meeting and formally thanking them for their time and help.

The Right Mentor for the Moment

The type of mentorship you need will change at different points in your career. My personal bias, that the right mentor is typically someone who is one to two levels above you in your current role, came from a gentleman who was a very senior executive at Cisco. He was speaking to a group of people who wanted to get into management, and shared, "Whatever you do, don't ask me to be your mentor. I'm a senior vice president and report to the CEO. I might tell you to go do things that could get you fired!" While he was joking (a bit), his feedback was spot on. A mentor who is currently in the next job you aspire to obtain, or the job after that, is going to have recent experience doing exactly what you want to do. They will be able to give you specific advice to help you get to the next level, whereas, if you go too high in your company hierarchy, your mentor won't be able to relate to the challenges that you're struggling with day to day. That doesn't mean there's no role in your life for a super-senior leader who thinks you're talented and has their eye on you … We'll talk a little more about advisors in chapter 10.

As I already mentioned, in a perfect world, your mentors shouldn't be in your reporting line. Of course it can work beautifully, but the best mentor-mentee relationships are the most open and honest ones, those where you have trust that you can say whatever you want to say, and your mentor will do the same. A girlfriend of mine recently told me she calls mentor hunting "looking for allies." Just looking for men and women that you respect and are respected in the company, and developing relationships with them can be game changing for your career.

Notice I said those allies can be either male or female. Women often want women mentors, because professional women have lived through the kinds of challenges I've been writing about in this book. However, I strongly believe excluding men from the role entirely can be a huge mistake. Perhaps you remember the book *Men Are from Mars, Women Are from Venus*, and I am here to tell you I agree. They're both great planets! Neither one is better than the other, but we are different from each other. We think differently. We process differently. And both ways of doing things are equally valid. So, especially if you aspire to reach the senior executive level ... and most of the senior executives in your company are men, you need to understand how they are thinking about things. As a woman, having male mentors like Doug was a game changer in my career because I learned to understand how he thought about problem solving, communication strategies, planning, execution, and more. I learned a lot.

I also think it's crucial, as you get promoted to being a leader, to pay it forward and make sure you are taking time to pick out your future leaders. When you see something special in someone, see someone doing more than they have to, acknowledge, "Wow, you're amazing, you did an outstanding job." Then offer to meet with them for thirty minutes, share you want to learn more from them, just like you would with a mentor. When you see someone who is bright, tap them on the shoulder and tell them, "You can do more. Let's get together." I've probably done that one hundred times throughout my career (but only if it was true!), because it's a win-win-win. Just as with hiring, when you recognize talented people and invest in them, it is valuable to them. It is valuable to you. And it is valuable to your company. You become known as the leader who builds amazing talent, just like our next Transformational Leader, Paula Hansen.

TRANSFORMATIONAL LEADER: PAULA HANSEN, PRESIDENT OF DOCUSIGN

Paula Hansen is the president and chief revenue officer (CRO) of Docusign, responsible for leading the global sales and partnerships organization, which includes worldwide sales, solutions consulting, and partners. With more than twenty-five years of leadership experience with high-growth market expansion, partner ecosystems, marketing, professional services, and customer success, she is passionate about customer experience and the role that data plays in driving meaningful business impact. Paula joined Docusign in August 2024 from Alteryx, where she served as president and chief revenue officer. Prior to Alteryx, she served as CRO of SAP Customer Experience and held various leadership roles at Cisco during her nineteen years with the company.

***

I've been fortunate to have many different mentors over my life and career, and one of the most pivotal mentors is the author of this book. I was inspired by Tracey's leadership style as a female executive, and by the fact that after leaving Cisco, she was running go-to-market organizations end to end at scale. She gave me courage to think that if she could be a president of a company, perhaps I could as well. I called Tracey at various times for advice throughout my career, including when I was evaluating job opportunities.

When I took my first role outside Cisco, I asked her guidance on how to approach the first ninety days. I had worked at Cisco for nineteen years and was worried about starting over and getting a fast start. Tracey gave me fantastic guidance about how to introduce myself to the new company, to articulate clearly why I joined in a way that inspired the team, and to put some operational elements in place early. Tracey urged me to spend time with top performers in the organization right away—asking them questions on what makes them successful. She suggested this because I could be a better leader if I knew the real skinny on what is working and what is not. To this day, I host roundtables with top performers and always think of her. Her advice on this, and so many other leadership practices, has helped me to be a more authentic and confident leader.

Three things I wish people had told me when I was starting out include the following:

1. **Know your strengths.** *Each of us has true strengths in how we work and lead—and they're often the skills that come most naturally to us. Consider how you create or process ideas, how you perform work, how you work with others, and how you communicate to help you find the best fit in your role and articulate your personal brand.*

2. **Know your areas of development.** *While you are playing to your strengths, you also need to identify where you can develop, improve, and gain new skills. This is normal—no one is perfect! Being able to articulate your development areas shows awareness and personal learning, and employees and managers value working with people who are self-aware. Keeping it real with yourself and others will make the journey better for you.*

3. **EQ trumps IQ.** *While IQ can carry you far, often EQ (emotional quotient) separates people in their career journeys. Sometimes called "soft" skills, I call EQ "being human" skills. EQ skills will help you to build relationships, empathize, defuse conflict, make decisions, manage stress, and ultimately reach your goals. Be authentic—be you!*

***

The right mentors can be great role models to help you develop your own leadership style. And yet, finding your own style can be a challenge for many due to the unconscious bias issues women face. We'll take a closer look at how to lead in a way that is effective while staying authentic to your true self in the next chapter.

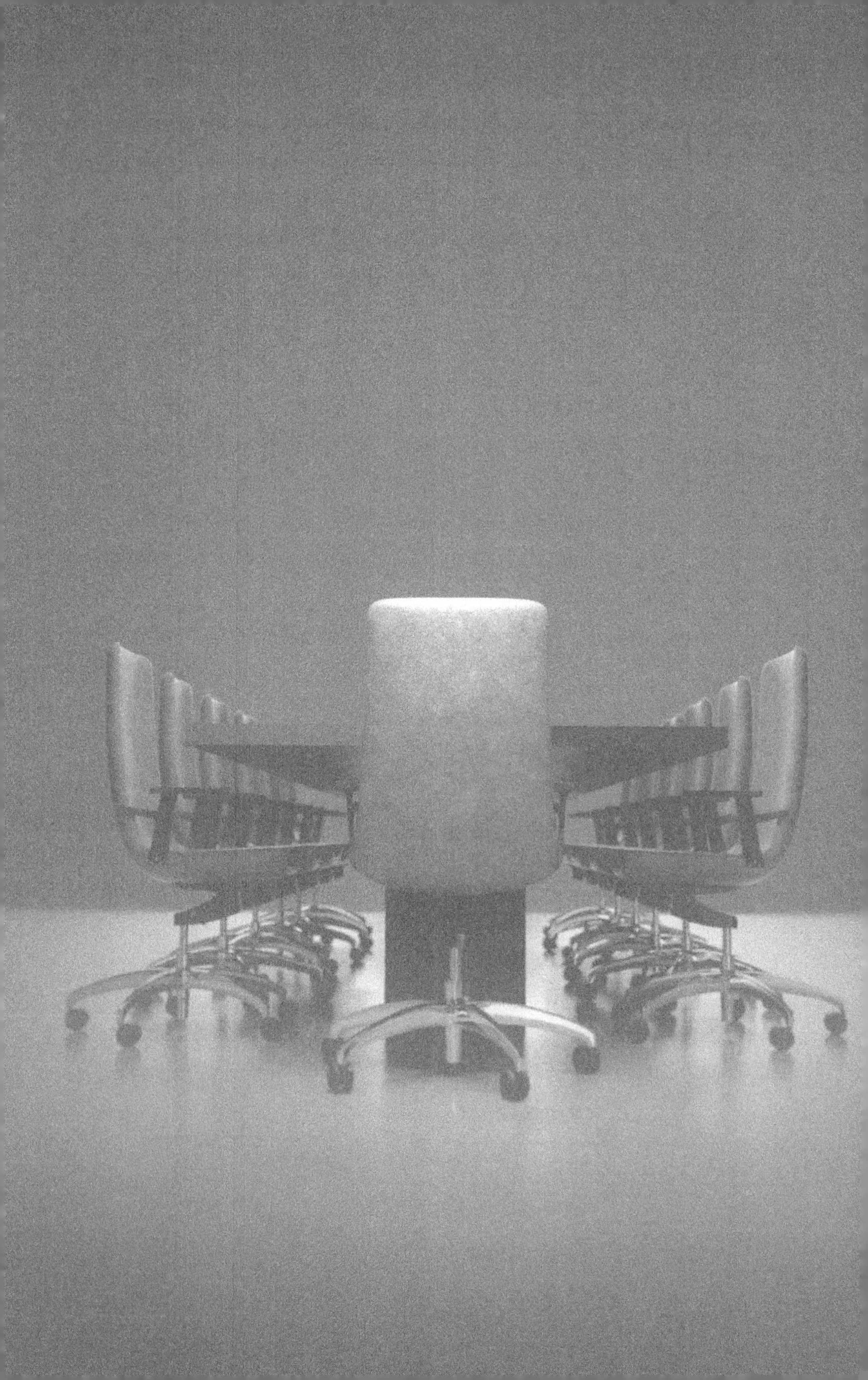

CHAPTER 9

Tough Enough?

I had just joined a new company, and one of my key team members was away on parental leave. When she came back to work for me, we got to know each other and became fast friends. After a while, she confessed that had not been her initial expectation of what our relationship would be like. "Back when I was on leave," she explained, "I told my husband, 'I think the new head of sales is a woman. I don't think I can come back and work for a woman!'"

We both started laughing that she had ever felt that way about me. "Really?" I asked her. "Seriously? We're supposed to support our fellow women leaders!"

"Believe me," she responded, "I've worked for some women in the past who were really difficult to work for."

She probably pictured me as some sort of tech version of Miranda Priestly in *The Devil Wears Prada*. If you've never seen the movie, Meryl Streep played the role of a demanding, impossible boss—she was completely uncompromising and was quick to call out publicly anyone who fell below her standards. Maybe my friend had worked for a boss like that before—and maybe you have too. There are, unfortunately, a lot of people who believe they literally have to fight their way to the top and are willing to push down anyone who gets in their way. Both men and women do this, but it's one of the most common stereotypes around female leaders—where unconscious bias suggests that women leaders are often assumed to be "too tough" or "not tough enough."

> **Unconscious bias suggests that women leaders are often assumed to be "too tough" or "not tough enough."**

The 2011 *Forbes* article "The 10 Worst Stereotypes about Powerful Women"[29] details the most common misconceptions about women in power that continue to hold us back. Reading through it, it looks like the screenwriters could have created the Miranda character just by referring to this list. I listed all those traits together so you'll see how clearly she embodies over half the stereotypes on the list, including these:

---

[29] Jenna Goudreau, "The 10 Worst Stereotypes about Powerful Women." *Forbes*, October 24, 2011, https://www.forbes.com/sites/jennagoudreau/2011/10/24/worst-stereotypes-powerful-women-christine-lagarde-hillary-clinton/.

ICE QUEEN
Women leaders are often perceived as cold and unapproachable, lacking warmth and empathy.

TOUGH AND AGGRESSIVE
Assertive women in leadership roles are frequently labeled as overly aggressive or domineering.

MASCULINE
Successful women are sometimes seen as having adopted traditionally male characteristics to succeed.

EMOTIONAL
Women leaders are often fairly characterized as being too emotional, suggesting they cannot make rational decisions.

QUEEN BEE
Powerful women are sometimes seen as unsupportive of other women, hoarding power and opportunities for themselves.

SINGLE AND LONELY
Successful women are stereotypically seen as sacrificing personal relationships and family life for their careers—in *The Devil Wears Prada*, Miranda is going through her second divorce.

Who wants to work for a boss like that? I know I wouldn't. Still, the remaining four stereotypes on *Forbes's* list may be even more dangerous, because they undermine women's authority, capability, and legitimacy as leaders. They are as follows:

INCOMPETENT

Despite their achievements, women in leadership roles often face skepticism about their competence and abilities.

WEAK

Despite the stereotype that women leaders are too tough, there is a contradictory stereotype that portrays us an inherently weaker and less capable of handling leadership pressures.

TOKEN

Successful women are sometimes dismissed as being tokens or filling a quota rather than being recognized for their skills and qualifications.

SEDUCTRESS

Some women leaders are sexualized and accused of using their sexuality to advance their careers.

I believe that stereotypes like these are one reason why so many women are afraid to pull their chair up to the table and take a seat. They don't want to be seen as pushy or aggressive, so they hide in the back row, often trying to be perfect in their role, hoping to be noticed. Unfortunately, that's not the way to have an impact in your organization, and it's definitely not the way to get you to the C-suite. So, how do you find the right balance, where you can lead confidently and authentically without giving the people who work for you nightmares?

Real Leadership

The good thing about the stereotypes about women leaders is that they are just that—*stereotypes*. There is a path to leading with assertiveness, authority, and empathy, as opposed to weakness or aggression. And it is very possible to be results oriented while still being a great collaborator.

I was in a Zoom meeting once when one of my engineering peers smiled and said, "The thing I love about you is you've got an iron fist, but it's in a velvet glove." I took this as such a compliment. I have always tried to position myself and any leader in my organization as "servant leaders," which is a philosophy that requires leaders to *help* make their teams as successful as possible.

Earlier I mentioned the television show the *Undercover Boss*, where CEOs and senior executives would go "under cover" (yes, literally dress in disguise) as entry-level employees to understand the problems in their companies. While I never did dress up, the "Undercover Boss" became one of my favorite strategies in leading teams. My goal was to figure out in a nonthreatening way what my people wanted and needed to make their jobs easier. I always spent a lot of time on the front line with my teams, working to understand the issues they faced, and then worked very hard to execute those changes inside the company. My goal was to be approachable and spend my time with *all* team members, not just my direct reports.

I want to be clear that servant leadership doesn't mean that results are optional. You can be collaborative and approachable, and yet, everyone needs to be clear on expectations. I am a big believer that in times of crisis, instability, or when people are simply worried, that's the time to be as calm as possible. But there are times when you have to be firm. Holding someone accountable isn't just good for you and your business; it's good for the person whose feet are being held to the fire. When you remind people that they aren't delivering, you are giving them a chance to improve.

I want to emphasize that all strategies did not always go according to plan, and I certainly wasn't always perfect as a people manager.

When I started my first role managing managers, we were successful, but in looking back, I've realized that the way I succeeded was by micromanaging my team. I may not have been Miranda Priestly, but I wasn't a lot of fun to work for, and by the end of a year, while our results were solid, I didn't feel good about the way we got there. I've often found I have learned more from my failures than my successes, and I soon changed and started putting into practice the principles that we're talking about in this book. I loosened up and involved my team in setting goals and strategy, and instead of slacking off, my team did even better. The plan became their plan. If I empowered my team, got them engaged, I could be more collaborative and less authoritative and still achieve outstanding results.

And yet, it's never easy when part of your job is telling someone they're not holding up their end of the bargain. Giving people tough feedback is one of the hardest pieces of the job, especially for new managers, but giving honest feedback is also one of the most important roles of a leader. Former Walmart CEO Lee Scott, known for his work in leading Walmart to be one of the best-performing stocks in the Dow Jones Industrial Average, included the ability to deliver feedback well as one of his ten principles of leadership success.[30] His ten principles are summarized below:

---

30 George Anderson, "Lee Scott's 10 Steps to Leadership Success," *RetailWire*, August 26, 2009, https://retailwire.com/discussion/lee-scotts-10-steps-to-leadership-success/.

CHAPTER 9

HIRING PEOPLE BETTER THAN YOURSELF.
Surrounding yourself with talented individuals makes it easier to achieve success.

REINING IN EGO.
Ego can be a significant impediment to effective leadership.

CLEAR COMMUNICATION.
Telling people what you want clearly often ensures you will receive it.

CONSTRUCTIVE FEEDBACK.
Providing others with honest and constructive feedback helps in their development.

UNDERSTANDING SELF-DOUBT.
Recognizing that most people feel they don't have everything under control can help in relating to and supporting your team.

EFFECTIVE LISTENING.
What is heard and how it is heard is often more important than what is said.

ADMITTING MISTAKES.
Being able to admit when you are wrong, even about things you feel strongly about, is crucial.

LISTENING TO CRITICS.
Sometimes harsh critics say things you need to hear for improvement.

SHARING PRAISE.
Give all the praise away to others, recognizing their contributions.

INTEGRITY.
Maintaining integrity is the most important principle in leadership.

I believe that more careers are ruined because the employee's manager is afraid to provide honest and constructive feedback to their employee regarding how they can improve. I haven't met many employees who join a company with the intent to fail. Our job as leaders, therefore, if we are hiring great people, is to coach our teams so they consistently improve to meet and exceed their goals. At least once per quarter, make time on your calendar to really think through one or two things each of your team members can work on to take their game to the next level. If the employee is doing a good job, but your feedback is to help them to reach the next level, tell them that so the feedback is delivered in a caring manner with the right tone. And if the employee is failing in their role, don't go it alone; be sure to enlist human resources and your boss to determine the best strategy and plan.

The other qualities Scott emphasized as essential—qualities like humility, effective communication, and integrity in leadership—are also critical, and research has proven women possess these in abundance. A Pew Research Center report found that qualities such as compassion and empathy, which are closely related to humility, are seen as strengths for women leaders.[31] The Zenger Folkman Crisis Leadership Study revealed that during the COVID-19 pandemic,

---

31 Juliana Menasce Horowitz, Ruth Igielnik, and Kim Parker, "Views on Leadership Traits and Competencies and How They Intersect with Gender," Pew Research Center, September 20, 2018, https://www.pewresearch.org/social-trends/2018/09/20/2-views-on-leadership-traits-and-competencies-and-how-they-intersect-with-gender/.

women leaders were found to be more effective, particularly in communication skills.[32] Another Zenger Folkman study showed that women scored "higher than men in most leadership skills."[33] That means that whoever you are, you most likely have all the tools you need to be an incredible leader right now. You don't need to fight your way every step up the ladder; you can be kind, nurturing, and approachable and still command the room. You owe it to yourself and the women in your organization to own your leadership style and be the authentic and effective leader your organization needs.

Say More and Say It Often

On that note, you also owe it to those women and to your organization to make sure you speak up. It breaks my heart when women ask me, "How can I get my voice heard?" as if this is often a challenge akin to climbing Everest. Your voice, your message, is critical to your company's success, so make sure you pull up that chair to the table. Are you going to make an impact right away? Maybe not. I can recall several times when I said "the sky was blue" in the conference room, and no one acknowledged my comment, only to have one of my male counterparts say exactly the same thing five minutes later, at which point everyone in the room would comment on his brilliant idea. When that happened, I didn't just accept it, but I didn't get angry either. Instead, I'd give everyone a big smile and say, "Didn't I just say

---

[32] Jack Zenger and Joseph Folkman, "Research: Women Are Better Leaders during a Crisis," Zenger Folkman, January 7, 2021, https://zengerfolkman.com/articles/research-women-are-better-leaders-during-a-crisis/.

[33] Jack Zenger and Joseph Folkman, "Research: Women Score Higher Than Men in Most Leadership Skills," *Harvard Business Review,* June 25, 2019, https://www.iwecfoundation.org/news/research-women-score-higher-than-men-in-most-leadership-skills-3/.

exactly that five minutes ago?" People would smile and laugh and say, "You did say that, didn't you?" It's important to be brave enough to ask for credit for your ideas. Eventually, people will catch on to the fact that you have relevant things to say.

Still, if you are being ignored all the time, you need to do something more concrete. For example, one comment I get a lot from women is, "There's ten men on the team plus my manager, and nobody listens to me." If that happens, my advice is to pull someone who was in the room at the time, someone that you trust, and just ask them offline, "What happened? What am I not doing that everyone else is doing in order to have my voice heard?"

When you go into a meeting, come prepared with your key thoughts. The first time I joined a board, I asked a mentor I really respected for advice. She told me that my goal for the meeting should be to make one good comment and ask one great question. I often share this advice with others, as my goal isn't to be the person who is talking all the time but to be seen as a thought leader, speaking when I have something to say that people need to hear.

Strong written and verbal communication skills are critical the higher you climb on the ladder. I recall we had a new president at one of my companies, and I noticed that whenever he spoke about what we needed to accomplish, he repeated himself at least eight times in company meetings, saying the same thing again and again consistently over time. It drove me a bit crazy, so I asked him about it. I said, "I've got it after one or two times. Why do you keep repeating yourself?"

He smiled and then explained that in general, people don't hear things the first or second or third time you say them, and if they do hear you the first few times, they are still questioning whether or not you're truly going to stick with the plan. "I intentionally will say things six, seven, or eight times," he said, "because I want people to know that yes, I'm serious, and we are really doing this. So, if you are going to be here, you need to get on board and do it too."

Developing a strong communication style is extremely important. I can't underscore enough the need for strong communication skills when you're trying to drive change, with a consistent cadence your team can rely on. And if you can add humor, while being vulnerable and authentic, that goes even further. Humor is natural for me, so find what's natural for you. That's the key. The greatest leaders aren't just exceptionally good at what they do; they accept other people, and more importantly, they accept themselves for who they are. You can't lead others to do their best work if you're constantly second-guessing yourself, so don't. Let go of the misconception that you have to present in a way that is different from your authentic self. Commit to standing by the person you are and allowing that person to lead. This is what your team and company need from you.

TRANSFORMATIONAL LEADER: LYNNE DOHERTY, PRESIDENT AND BOARD MEMBER

Lynne Doherty is the president of field operations at Sonar, a company known for its clean code solutions that help developers improve code quality and security. In her role, Lynne oversees global sales, demand generation, customer success, and support teams. She joined Sonar in 2024 after serving as the president of worldwide field operations at Sumo Logic, where she played a pivotal role in optimizing the go-to-market strategies for operational scale and speed. Lynne brings over twenty years of experience in sales leadership, including significant roles at McAfee and Cisco.

***

I was in a senior position at a big company when an announcement came out that one of our colleagues had been promoted into an even bigger, more important job. The announcement went on to say that everyone knew this person as "the nicest person we know." I immediately thought to myself, "Nice" is not the first word I want someone to describe me with when thinking about me in a professional context.

Fast-forward and I was with a group of VPs who worked for me, and I actually made an offhanded comment that I wouldn't want "nice" to be the first word that someone said about me. They all laughed and said, "Lynne, you have nothing to worry about." They meant it as a compliment—we had a really good relationship, and they expanded on the comment to clarify that I was nice, but their first words about me would be "smart" or "driven" or "sets a high bar." That's what I wanted. To me, calling a professional woman "nice" is similar to someone telling you your blind date has a "good personality." It suggests there aren't any other good qualities to call out.

If you're concerned about how you're showing up at work, here are my suggestions:

1. **You're always a role model for someone, whether you know it or not, especially as a woman.** *Thirty years ago, very early in my career, I was literally the only woman selling into financial services in New York. I would spend all my time speaking about sports, the stock market, or business, and I put a box around anything that felt personal or feminine. Then my boss's boss's boss, a woman who was known for being very tough,*

came to town for a meeting with a sales rep who worked for me. The meeting was only supposed to be thirty minutes, but they were gone for more than two hours … and when they finally walked in, the sales rep was carrying six bags of Ferragamo shoes! It turned out my boss's boss's boss was from Boston, where they don't have Ferragamo stores, so when she spotted one, they went shopping. This story shaped how I showed up from that moment on. I saw that you can hold people to a high standard and love nice shoes at the same time. You can be authentic.

2. **You can also be truthful and kind at the same time.** *And you should be. If you're kind but not truthful, that's not good, and if you're truthful but unkind, that's unacceptable as well.*

3. **Intent matters.** *When you give hard feedback, do it because you care, because you want the recipient to be successful. Push them to do more because you know that they can achieve next-level accomplishments. You don't have to be tough for the sake of being tough.*

Once you master your leadership style, you will begin to build the skills you'll need on your path to the C-suite. However, there may be times when all your hard work seems to be getting you nowhere. We'll explore some strategies for what to do when you hit a ceiling in the next chapter.

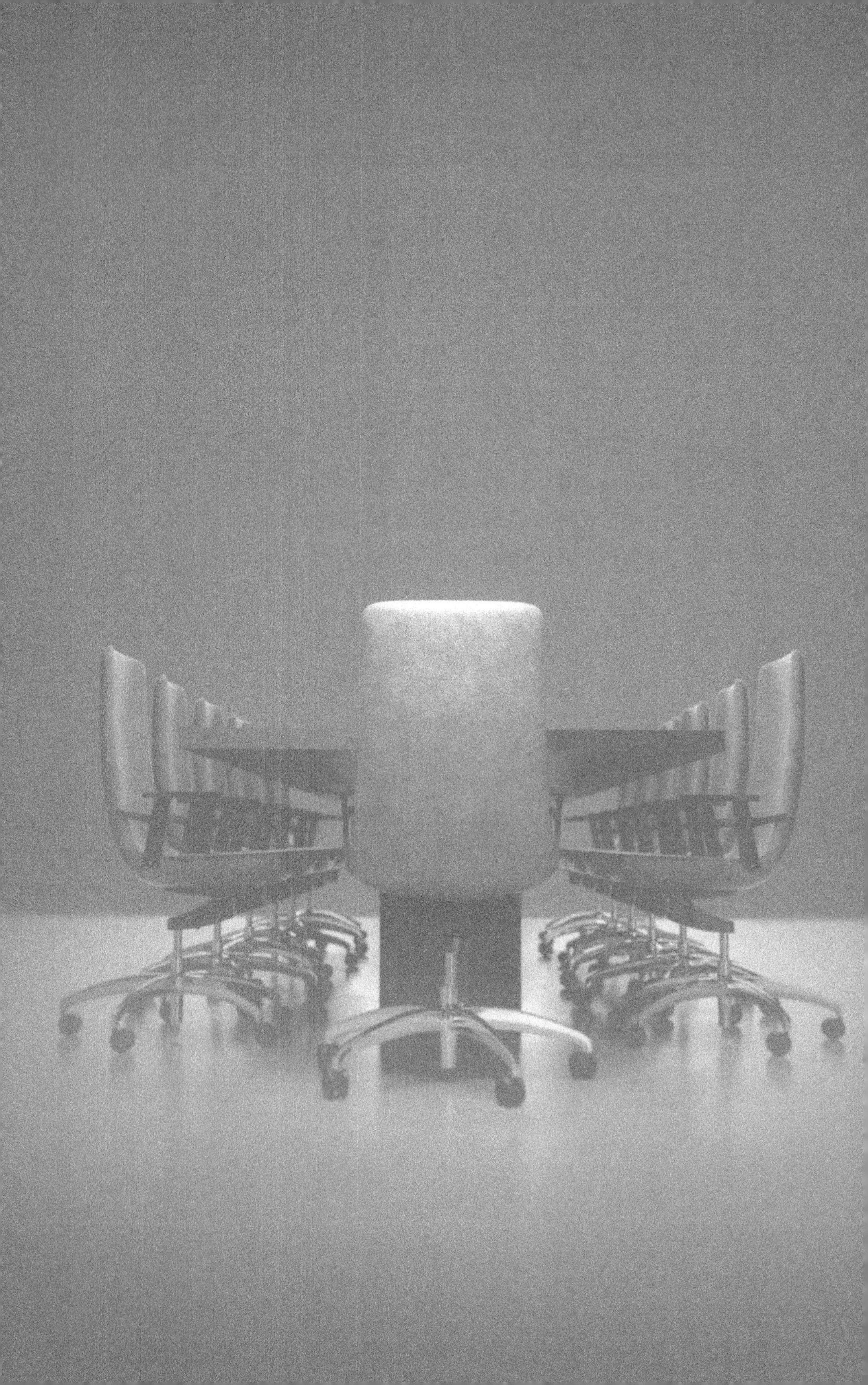

CHAPTER 10

Hitting a Ceiling

I was an area vice president for Cisco Systems, running a very large business. It was an important job, and I had done well in the role, but I still felt stuck. Every day was a different version of the day before. While my team was doing great, I felt as though I wasn't learning anything new. I could feel a sense of "smoldering discontent" building (that same feeling I felt back when I wanted to quit my job earlier on). I was older and wiser—I knew I didn't want to leave the company—but I also knew a promotion to a senior vice president role was a long way off. There were many amazing AVPs in line with me.

I had hit a ceiling.

So, what did I do? I took a "lateral" role.

Cisco had just purchased a company called Webex, at a time when SaaS, or software as a service, was a new idea. Our CEO called it one of the most strategic acquisitions the company had ever made. So, I kept my title as a vice president, but my area was now expanded into running worldwide sales for Webex. And suddenly I was learning again like never before.

That sense of discontent I'd had as an area vice president was always my red flag that it was time to take a hard look at my situation, take stock of my options, and see what new challenges were available to me. For me, in that particular moment, and maybe for you if you're feeling stuck in your current role, the best option can often come in the form of a lateral move. I know it may not be what you want. It's natural to gravitate toward the bigger title and the better pay package that come with getting promoted. But honestly, sometimes those things are far less important to your development than a position that offers a real opportunity to learn, grow, and increase your skills and experiences. A lateral move may be the exact jump start your career needs. I've known many men and women who were "stuck" in a role, and an old boss suggested a lateral job change; fast-forward twelve to eighteen months, and that promotion came through for them due to their increased experience.

The Importance of Advisors

Notice I mentioned the idea to make a lateral move often came from *an old boss*. The people you've worked for and learned from over the years, the people you've gotten to know and admire, can and should continue to play an important role in your professional life. When you hit a ceiling or some other crisis point where you really don't know what to do, that's the time to turn to your advisors—people who know you well, are invested in your success, and are willing to tell you the hard-to-hear truth to help you get where you're trying to go.

There is a lot of current research and discussion about CEOs having a "personal board of directors," referring to an informal group of trusted individuals who provide guidance, feedback, and support, similar to what a formal board of directors does for a corporation.

We're going to be talking about a company's board of directors a bit later in this book, so to avoid any confusion, I'm going to avoid the term and refer to your individuals as your board of advisors.

CEOs choose advisors to offer diverse perspectives and expertise, help them navigate complex decisions, provide honest feedback, and support their personal and professional growth. According to the *Harvard Business Review*, they help the individuals they advise stay accountable while challenging their thinking and providing critical feedback.[34] The right advisors can help you manage stress, make better decisions, and improve your leadership skills, acting as a sounding board for ideas and providing insights you might not have considered otherwise. As a result, CEOs who engage with a personal advisory group tend to perform better and are better at navigating challenges like cultural alignment and talent management within their organizations.[35]

So, the next step in this journey is for you to identify and start to engage with your own trusted advisors.

While advisors are *similar* to mentors, they are not the same thing. Mentors are generally best suited to helping you achieve short-term goals, like rising to the next level or two within your organization. Generally, advisors are there to help with big-picture items and your long-term career goals, although they can also give great short-term advice that keeps your long-term goals in mind. A mentor can certainly morph into an advisor over time. Advisors tend to be people who (a) really know you, what you're capable of, and what your dreams are and (b) are willing to invest some of themselves in

---

[34] Carolyn Dewar, Martin Hirt, and Scott Keller, "The Mindsets and Practices of Excellent CEOs," McKinsey & Company, October 25, 2019, https://www.mckinsey.com/capabilities/strategy-and-corporate-finance/our-insights/the-mindsets-and-practices-of-excellent-ceos.

[35] "Measure of Leadership: CEOs and Directors on Navigating Change," SpencerStuart, June, 2024, https://www.spencerstuart.com/research-and-insight/measure-of-leadership-ceos-and-directors-on-navigating-change.

helping you get there. They can be people one or two levels or greater above what you aspire to be, inside or outside your company, but as with mentors, ideally, not in your reporting chain so that there's no conflict of interest and no worries about being completely honest.

Honesty is crucial to these relationships; you need to understand why you're not "getting that promotion" or whatever your challenge is that you're facing. I would always tell my own advisors, "I need honest feedback, always, and don't worry—you're going to have to work really hard to hurt my feelings." It can be done, of course, but what I am looking for from my advisors is constructive feedback as to what's working and what's not. At the same time, you need to be comfortable being honest with your advisors. You need to be able to tell them what you aspire to do over time so they can help you drill down to what you should be doing over the next twelve or eighteen months to prepare for the next promotion.

An executive coach can also be an advisor. Sometimes your company will hire one for you, and if they do, that's a great sign. It means they really believe in you, and they're willing to invest in you. You can also hire your own executive coach, which can be especially helpful when you need help working through a thorny problem like hitting a ceiling or coping with a difficult manager. When you work with a coach, they're not listening to you because they're doing you a favor; it's their actual job. So, you can demand more time and attention if the situation calls for it.

The Advisor/Advisee Relationship

In addition to being people who know you well (with the exception of professional coaches, who are paid to get to know you well), your advisors, ideally, should be people who are well respected and individuals you aspire to be like long term. The goal is to draw from a long range of perspectives, and for that you need a mix of different types of people—they can include peers as well as people who are a few levels above you, people in your function or in different functional roles. But mostly, look for people whose opinions you value who are willing to tell you the truth. This is not about finding cheerleaders to pump you up by saying how terrific you are. You're looking for people who can see what you don't see and are actually willing to tell you.

Once you've identified someone as a potential advisor, approach them the same way you would approach a potential mentor. Asking, "Hey, can we spend some time together?" or "Can I buy you a coffee?" is a good, low-pressure way to start. Also as with mentorship, you will have to control the agenda. You can't just show up at your meeting and say, "Hey, I'm here. Where do I need to get better?" Be specific as to what you want to get out of each conversation. Begin by sharing your North Star and talking about what you hope to accomplish over the course of your career. Tell this potential advisor what it is that drew you to them, and where you think they can help. Let them know what you're looking for, what you're bumping up against, then ask them for some feedback.

For example, imagine you're feeling stuck and keep getting passed over for that promotion. You might start by asking your advisor to rank you in the following areas:

1. Executive presence
2. Setting strategy
3. Problem solving
4. Communications
5. Creating results

At the end, if the meeting goes well and there's good dialogue, you might say, "Hey, I am trying to informally build a small group of advisors that can help me reach my long-term goals. Would you be willing to meet with me once per quarter or twice per year?" The frequency will naturally be less than a mentor's meeting, as these advisors are there for big-picture issues, long-term goal setting, and strategy and planning—timing can change based upon where you are in your career. And unless they're really busy, most people are going to say yes.

Once your advisor helps you define where your gaps are, take two or three of those gaps to your manager and their manager and share what you've learned: "These are a few areas I believe I should work on. Do you agree? What is missing to help me land the next promotion?" This will (hopefully) bring your managers on board and make them part of the process too.

Set quarterly or biannual one-on-one meetings with your advisor, but again, the frequency will be less often than check-ins with a mentor and most likely more fluid based upon what is going on in your life at the time. If an advisor is inside your company and more senior than you, you can offer them your own insights around what is working and what is not inside their organization of the company to help keep them grounded. As I discussed earlier, I learned so much from my mentees, who were often closest to the customer, advising them to please tell me what was truly working as it related to my initiatives and assuring them that they were now in my "Witness Protection Program" so they knew I would always protect whatever they shared as anonymous feedback. Consider being a part of your advisor's Witness Protection Program (if they have one) to help with where their initiatives are working, and ideas to make them stronger.

The main thing you can offer back is feedback and reminders. Reiterate what you covered in your last discussion, tell your advisor what you implemented and how it worked, and of course, thank them. Let them know they're not wasting their time and that you are taking their feedback seriously. Given your advisor had help along the way, too, your advisor won't expect much more than this.

TRANSFORMATIONAL LEADER: DEBBIE MCCLURE, GLOBAL HEAD OF SALES AT DROPBOX

A career sales professional with more than thirty years in the technology sector with experience in all aspects of the selling world, Deb has been involved in selling across multiple verticals and technologies from the Fortune 10 to small business entities. She is an accomplished sales leader who began her career as an individual contributor and worked her way through multiple sales leadership positions. Debbie has led teams in multiple facets of sales including outside and digital sales teams, services sales, and sales operations. Prior to Dropbox, Deb spent twenty years at Cisco, where she led the sales and engineering teams responsible for Cisco's service provider segment in the Americas sales organization. Deb came to Dropbox in January 2021 and has been instrumental in reinvigorating the global sales organization.

***

I remember the first time I got stuck. I was a first-line leader and wanted to get promoted to a second-line leader, and I went to one of my advisors, who was also one of the company's senior vice presidents, for advice. He told me, "It's clear that you can sell and you can lead sales teams, but as you go up in the organization, you really need operational muscle." They recommended that I do a rotation into sales operations, and so I did. And I learned a lot.

I also got held up by refusing to, as I saw it, "play the political game" and talk up my accomplishments, because I thought it was inauthentic. I felt that I should prove myself with the work that I did and that other people would recognize that work. But then someone on my board of advisors told me, "It's really not about you, it's about them. Senior leaders are too busy to know what you're doing, and if you're doing good things that can help them scale, they want to know about it. Not sharing is actually inauthentic on your part." That advice flipped the tables for me. It helped me to understand that telling my senior leaders about my accomplishments was not about playing a game or "managing up,"—it was actually sharing what was working in my team so my boss could then help other teams across the company. My board of advisors has been so valuable in giving me feedback and coaching, which has really accelerated my career growth.

If you're hoping to engage a board that will be equally helpful, here are my best suggestions:

1. **Go for diversity.** *Ideally, you want a range of perspectives represented on your board, provided each individual member is also a person you trust, respect, and have an ongoing relationship with. Advisors should also be people who "have done this before" and will give you advice you know you can trust.*

2. **Cultivate different types of support.** *In addition to advisors, you will need sponsors and mentors in your professional career. Understand the different dynamics between these different types of support and how to leverage each of them strategically.*

3. **Always advocate.** *Always speak up for yourself about where you want to go, and proactively seek advice on how to get to the next position, whether that be up the ladder or to the side on the corporate jungle gym.*

In the spirit of keeping it real, part of working with your advisors will be figuring out, *Is my manager on board with supporting me and my career goals?* If over time, you and your advisors agree that you and your manager aren't connecting for whatever reason, you might need to look for a different role. The result could mean considering a lateral move to another team, to include cross-functional opportunities, where you'll be better supported. If that doesn't work and you're truly not making progress, it may be time to move to another company. We'll talk about what to do when you hit that kind of ceiling in our next chapter.

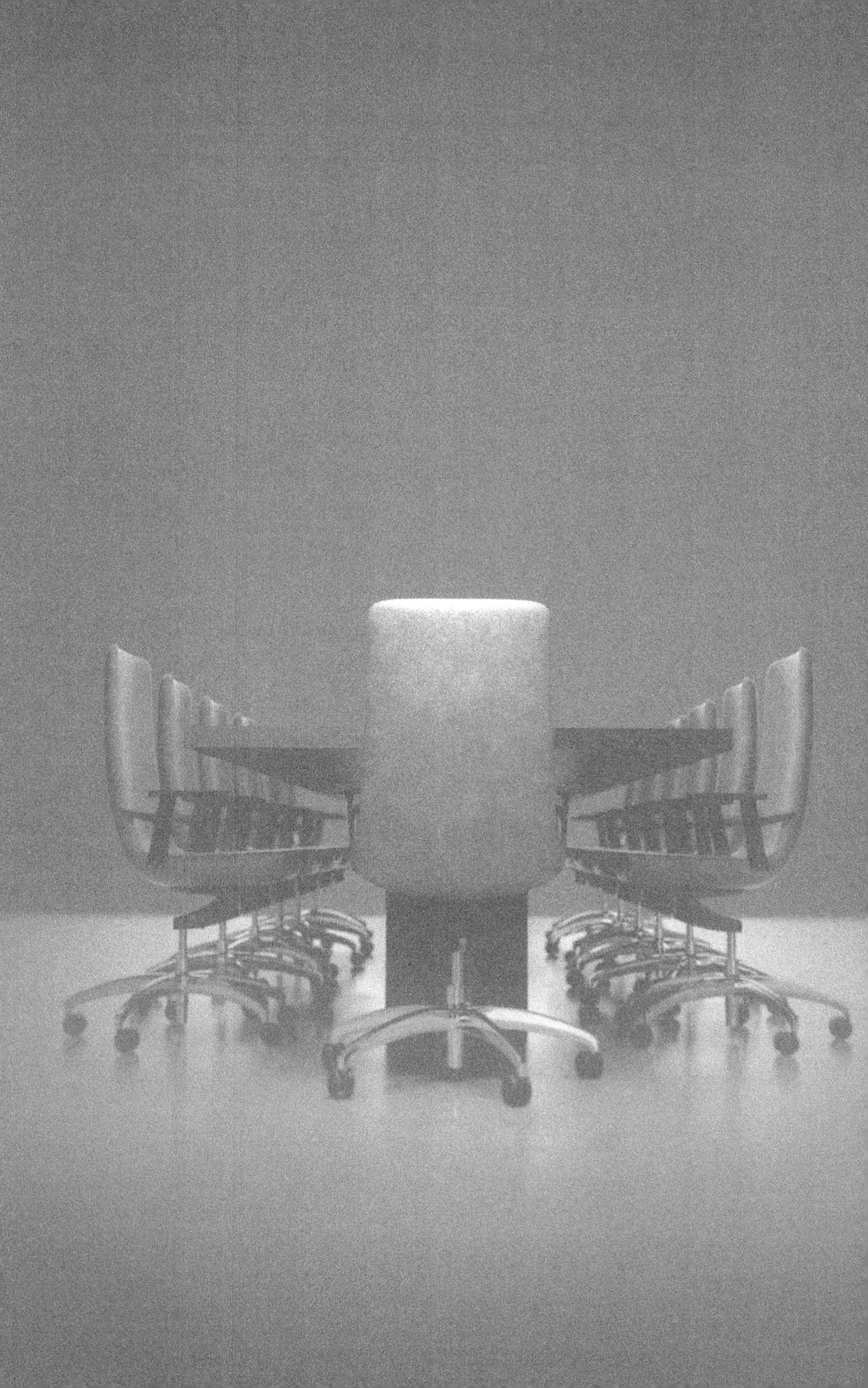

CHAPTER 11

Moving On

For a good portion of my career, whenever I switched companies, I followed people. I moved from place to place, often because an old boss or a friend worked there. This is the way many people switch companies and build their careers, which isn't necessarily a bad thing. But it isn't necessarily a good thing either. I've seen countless situations where a great leader brings ten or one hundred people on board, and then promptly leaves the company. Suddenly, those ten or one hundred people find themselves stranded in a situation they didn't sign up for. If you're intent on forging a path to the C-suite, getting marooned in a position like this can be a frustrating detour.

It was for this reason, later in my career, I decided I was going to approach things differently. You see, I was in a very challenging industry and knew it was time to make a career change. And as I reflected on my career decisions in the past, I noticed that I, too, had been following leaders who I knew and trusted. But even great leaders can make mistakes on the companies they choose, and so I decided I was going to try a new approach. I sought counsel from one of my advisors, Kelly O. Kay, Global Managing Partner, Software Practice at Heidrick & Struggles, one of the top executive search firms in the world. I'll never forget his advice:

"You want to talk yourself *out* of the job, not *into* the job."

What exactly does that mean? Well, like most people, when I had accepted previous roles, I'd naturally focused on all the exciting parts of my potential new job and company. Kelly advised me to slow down. Every role will face difficulties, and you need to understand what those challenges truly are before you accept a new job.

Kelly told me to open an Excel spreadsheet and, in the first column, list all my criteria for the company I wanted to work for. He wanted specifics. What size company did I want to go to? A $100 million company or a $10 billion company? What attributes did I want in the CEO? What kind of industry did I want to be working in? What kind of product did I want to sell? Where did I want the headquarters to be located, and was it important for that location to be close to me? The conversation went on and on like this. It was, as I said, critical to be clear on what my perfect role and company looked like *before* I started interviewing with other companies.

> "You want to talk yourself *out* of the job, not *into* the job."

Once I had my criteria down, my next step was to list every company that fit those parameters across the top of the spreadsheet. This became my criteria for evaluating all the companies I wanted to consider. One by one, I started reaching out to companies (and recruiters) to set up meetings. I always advise people to try to "kiss a hundred frogs," meaning if you're planning a career change, ensure you look at as many companies as you can. I probably evaluated fifty companies when I was making a change. It was overwhelming at first, but after a while, it became much easier. The more people I talked to and the more companies I looked at, the clearer it became as to what I wanted (and didn't want) my next role and my next company to look like. I reached a point where I was able to decide an opportunity was not the right role for me without even speaking to the recruiter. (But I *always* called the recruiters back—more on this later.)

Eventually, I landed at a $100 million company where I knew there was a lot of work that needed to be done—which also fit exactly with the criteria I had determined I wanted by using Kelly's process. Five years later, our revenue had grown to over $700 million, and the company is over $2 billion today. We had a very good run.

The Power of Negative Thinking

Why on earth, when you're trying to find a new job, should you be actively trying to talk yourself out of a role that might sound great? First of all, because every recruiter and management team you're working with is doing their darndest to talk you *into* that job. Any job you're interviewing for is going to be ten times harder than the recruiter is telling you. This is why they are hiring you—there are problems to be solved! So you need to do your due diligence. I often would share with the CEO or hiring manager that I wanted to know where all the bodies were buried to ensure I could indeed do a great job for the company, encouraging the team to give me the good, bad, and ugly as to the requirements of the role. Reviewing old quarterly business reviews is a great way to understand the challenges as well as to explore with the hiring manager how you might tackle some of the challenges that need to be solved. Look around the corners and do everything you can to talk yourself out of that job.

And yes, you should do this even if you're desperate to get out of your current role. I have been there, too, and would advise that this is a time when you need to be the most cautious. The last thing you want to do is jump from the frying pan into the fire. Moving from a job that you're unhappy in, to a job that you're miserable in can (and does!) happen if you forget to truly look before you leap. Instead of heading to the C-suite, it is not unheard of to become one of those job hoppers, which we're all trying to avoid.

So, if you're feeling anxious, take a deep breath. Remind yourself that this is the time to be even more thoughtful and analytical. Work to talk yourself out of whatever job you're considering, not because you won't ultimately take it, but because if and when you do, you'll do so with an understanding of exactly what you're getting into. Almost every company has issues that need to be resolved. The goal for you is to know what those issues are, and whether you can, and want to, help solve them.

Setting Your Criteria

When you're in a job that you don't like, when you're generally unhappy, or even when you just feel ready for change, most people tend to focus on getting a new job. I am here to advise you that you don't simply want a *new* job—you want a new *amazing* job. And for that, you need to remember your North Star. What is that big outrageous goal you're trying to reach? Is this really the right job to keep you on the path toward getting there? This is why having clear criteria (in writing!) is so important.

> **I am here to advise you that you don't simply want a *new* job—you want a new *amazing* job.**

Over time, my criteria became very clear. For starters, I knew I wanted to work in a critical market category, and unless you're a glutton for punishment, I would recommend the same for you. No matter what your function—sales, engineering, marketing, human resources—if the company is in a difficult market category, it's most likely going to be a tough job. If a company is having a hard time meeting its revenue goals, every function will most likely face challenges. Oftentimes, the result can end in cost cutting, layoffs, and morale issues. So, ask yourself: *Is it a relevant and important market? Are you excited about their mission? Is the product differentiated? Is the product something that is a "must-have" or a "nice to have"?*

In analyzing companies, I also look for companies that are in high-growth mode. In her book *Lean In*,[36] Sheryl Sandberg made a big impression on me when discussing her decision to join Google, which, at the time, was nowhere near the tech giant it is today. She had big offers with prestigious titles from plenty of bigger, more established companies, but she went with Google because she saw potential. She saw a chance to grow with a company on the cutting edge of something new and possibly be part of something transformative. Would the whole world know the name Sheryl Sandberg if she'd taken one of those other positions? We'll never know. But we do know that her strategy, which culminated in her being named Facebook's COO and a thought leader with almost unparalleled influence, paid off.

I will admit I was told several times by executive search firms when I made the decision to join a growth company that had only $100 million in revenue that I was making a big mistake. I was told I was supposed to be running large software companies, not "going for growth" as I intended. Don't get me wrong: large companies offer sophisticated, cutting-edge training programs and really high-quality, experienced management teams, many of whom have been there for years. My experience in large companies provided me with an incredi-

---

36   Sheryl Sandberg, *Lean In: Women, Work, and the Will to Lead* (Knopf, 2013).

ble foundation of knowledge that served me for decades, while helping me build a powerful network of support across my industry. But once the skill sets I absorbed at those big companies were embedded in me, I gravitated toward smaller and smaller organizations, because that's where I could leverage those skills to have the biggest impact.

For you, your motivators may be different. Working in large companies can provide an equally lucrative career track with many, many paths to success. The important thing is to be able to define what is important to you as you launch your search.

Do also consider whether you prefer to work for a public company or a private company, and if you prefer a private company, whether you are more interested in venture capital–backed or private equity–backed companies, because the dynamics in all these different structures are different. Consider the type of CEO you want to work for. Personally, I gravitate toward founders, but you may have other preferences. Glassdoor is a great place to get the inside scoop on a company's leadership team and culture and an overall feel for a company's strengths, as well as their trials and tribulations.

Some of my other criteria focus on a company's culture. I like to work for companies that have a customer-centric culture, because I believe that when you put the customer first, good things tend to happen. But again, these are just a few of my criteria. You're not going to know all these details going in, and that's okay. After you've been through ten or fifteen of these conversations, you will get clearer and clearer on what matters to you and what's a deal breaker. Once you reach that point—when you're clear on your criteria—you can start rating the companies you consider. I like to use a one to five scale, with five being high and one being low.

Getting Started

If the idea of vetting fifty to a hundred companies as a strategy sounds a little daunting, don't panic. This is another thing you can absolutely plan for and work into your schedule without a lot of disruption. Remember how we talked earlier about how what gets on your calendar gets done? What I used to do is create a code name for my job search—something that wouldn't arouse any suspicion if someone were to walk in my office and see it on my calendar—and schedule at least thirty minutes to an hour, at least once a week. I would spend that time prospecting for new roles.

Lining up all those companies to consider isn't something you must do alone—you need allies. You probably have friends who work or have worked for companies that you're interested in. Let them know what sort of opportunity you're looking for and ask if their company is hiring. Ask what recruiters they know and if they can introduce you so it's a warm introduction. Get the word out and put your network to work for you, just like you would (and do) for them. After a month or so, your flywheel will be rolling.

Once you meet a recruiter, nurture these relationships. A practice of mine is to always respond when a recruiter calls or emails me, and I keep all the notes from our meetings when they come in. Why? Because I never know when I might need that person's help. If someone contacts me with a job that doesn't sound like it fits my criteria, I will reply, "This probably isn't the right role for me, but I'm happy to jump on a call to understand more about what you're looking for and share my network with you."

When you have a couple of interactions like this with a recruiter, they're going to want to know more about you. They will ask for your specific criteria and update their database accordingly, which will lead to more quality referrals for you and more opportunities for you to refer others. I know from experience that this is how you build strong, long-lasting relationships with executive search teams that will be loyal to you for years to come. It has been a key strategy for me in playing the long game and building my career. When you have executive search teams on your side, they'll do anything for you, whether it's finding you your dream job, introducing you to the employee who will take your team to the next level … or yes, even talking you out of making a bad choice with the wrong company! (And you'll develop some lifelong friendships along the way as well.)

Your "Pitch"

You also need to be ready to seize opportunities when they come. You never know when or where you might meet the right person, so it's important to have your three-to-five-minute elevator pitch down. You want it to be succinct, you want it to be compelling, and you definitely want it to be well practiced.

A good elevator pitch doesn't need to be complicated—in fact, it shouldn't be. I break it down into two parts. The first one or two minutes should focus on who you are, like a highlight reel of your CV, and the second half should focus on what you want. For example, this is the first half of my elevator pitch:

"Hi, my name's Tracey Newell. I grew up at large companies including AT&T and Cisco, and from there I decided to go to smaller organizations. I joined Juniper Networks, which was about a $3.5 billion company at the time, where I was responsible for a billion-dollar business. Our company wanted a relationship with Polycom, and I shared that I'd help build an alliance between our two companies. Sixty days later, I was an officer for Polycom, which was a $1.2 billion company. What I learned throughout these changes was that the smaller the company was becoming, the more fun I was having. So, I joined a smaller public company called Proofpoint that was approximately $100 million, and we grew to $700 million in five years. From there, I knew I wanted to do board work. I gained my first board role when I was approached by Informatica. We got along so well that after two years they asked me to step off the board and join the management team."

That's the "who I am" portion. Short and sweet. Next, I spend another two minutes or so describing what I want, which sounds like a slightly longer version of this:

"What I am looking for is a board seat for a high-growth company. I love working with CEOs who are founders, with a must-have product in a critical industry that's growing at least 30 percent a year. I am also looking for CEOs and management teams who genuinely want help and engagement from their board members, as I have a lot of energy to help them get to the next level."

Honestly, that's really all there is to it: this is who I am (and what my qualifications are) and what I'm looking for. A lot of people make it harder than it has to be, rambling on about everything they've ever done or any job they might possibly consider. You don't need to do that. Get a crisp pitch that makes those two things clear. I laughingly share that someone should be able to wake you up at two in the morning and you can immediately repeat "your pitch" word for word. It will really help both you and the search teams helping you to find your dream job.

Job Hunting on the Down-Low

Job hunting while you have a job can feel awkward. When I began my search for what would ultimately be that pivotal role in a $100 million company, I was convinced word was going to get out. I was an officer in a large public company. I had a board; I had many influential people around me—how could they not know? But the thing is, they didn't. Over the course of my career, I have been pleasantly surprised to discover that in any job search, recruiters, executive teams, and managers all understand the need for strict confidentiality. I worried about being found out—a lot—but there truly does seem to be a confidentiality code that people stick by. And it makes sense. If there wasn't, no one would ever take the risk of interviewing unless there was no other option!

Still, because I was so worried, I also had a plan B. It was very straightforward: I was always very forthright with my boss about my ambition and the fact that I wanted to do more. "I've been in this job for two or three years," I would periodically remind them. "What's my next opportunity? I am eager to move forward and take on more responsibility; can we create a plan?" One of the rules I've tried to live by is to never surprise my manager if I was unhappy and looking for change. That way, if my boss called me in and said, "Hey, I hear you're interviewing," I could be honest and say, "Look, I can't control what people are saying about me, but as I have shared with you, I do want to get promoted. I would love to work on that plan with you." And I would also add, "I also want you to know that I am spending all of my energy making sure that I'm doing a really great job in this role." My goal was to let them know that I might be taking calls from recruiters periodically, without giving them cause for any action other than to help me if they wanted me to stay with the company.

But again, I never needed to do that, because no one revealed my secrets. And my hope is that when you're looking for your next amazing job, you won't have a problem either. Our next Transformational Leader, aviation pioneer Stephanie Chung, shares her insights.

TRANSFORMATIONAL LEADER: STEPHANIE CHUNG, FORMER PRESIDENT OF JETSUITE

Stephanie Chung is a trailblazer in the aviation industry, celebrated as the first African American to lead a private jet company, JetSuite. Beginning her career as a ground handler in the airline industry, she rose through the ranks to become a Transformative Leader, later serving as chief growth officer for Wheels Up. With over thirty years of experience in strategic innovation and business growth, Stephanie has driven remarkable successes at companies like American Airlines, Flexjet, and Bombardier Aerospace. Her leadership at JetSuite earned the company accolades including "Best Places to Work" and as one of *Dallas Business Journal*'s 100 Fastest Growing Private Companies. Stephanie is a dedicated advocate, serving on the Make-A-Wish board and the National Business Aviation Association's advisory council. She has been honored as one of *Adweek*'s Women Trailblazers and *Ebony*'s Power 100, with her influence extending globally as a sought-after keynote speaker. Stephanie is also the author of the number one international bestseller *Ally Leadership: How to Lead People Who Are Not Like You.*

***

I grew up knowing I wanted to be in aviation, but I had never seen a person of color depicted as an aviator. Still, I knew what I wanted to do, so I skipped college and got a job as a ground handler, parking planes and loading luggage, because I wanted to get my foot in the door. I knew I could prove myself from there, and I did. I was recruited into sales and built my dream career as an airline executive.

When the private jet industry came knocking, I told the recruiter, "I don't know anything about private jets." I was pretty sure I'd never seen a private jet. Still, it sounded like an interesting challenge—to do what I already knew how to do, which was driving sales for an airline, for this interesting growing sector, serving this elite market of movers and shakers. I knew I would learn a ton. I also knew I would be taking a risk and that I had to come to grips with—and release—how I saw my life playing out. And when I did take that risk, it opened the door to endless possibilities.

If you're hoping your next move leads to endless possibilities for you, here is my advice:

1. **Do your research.** *Look at the company, the position, the pros and cons. Ask yourself,* Where do I want to go? What kind of company do I want to work for? What do I bring to the table? *But also, think about what you like to do and what you love about your job. After twenty years in aviation, I reached a career crossroads and started thinking,* What do I want to do next? *I did a pros and cons list and realized that what I loved most about my job was coaching and mentoring people. I decided to take another risk and leave the private jet industry and open my own coaching and consulting practice, and I absolutely loved it.*

2. **Take risks.** *Once your research is done, don't be afraid of taking risks. If you make a bad decision, none of this stuff is going to kill you, so why not try it? And remember this:*

3. **There's always another job out there.** *If you're good at what you do and something doesn't work out, maybe it just wasn't the right fit. You can always go back to a place where you're more comfortable and simply change things up.*

Whether you're changing jobs or moving to a new company, remember, don't just follow people from place to place. Take time to define the specific kind of environment you want to work in and look at every company that fits your parameters to find the best opportunity for you to achieve your goals. In our next segment, we'll look at where this kind of smart career planning can lead when we explore what happens behind the closed doors of the boardroom—and how you can get them to open for you.

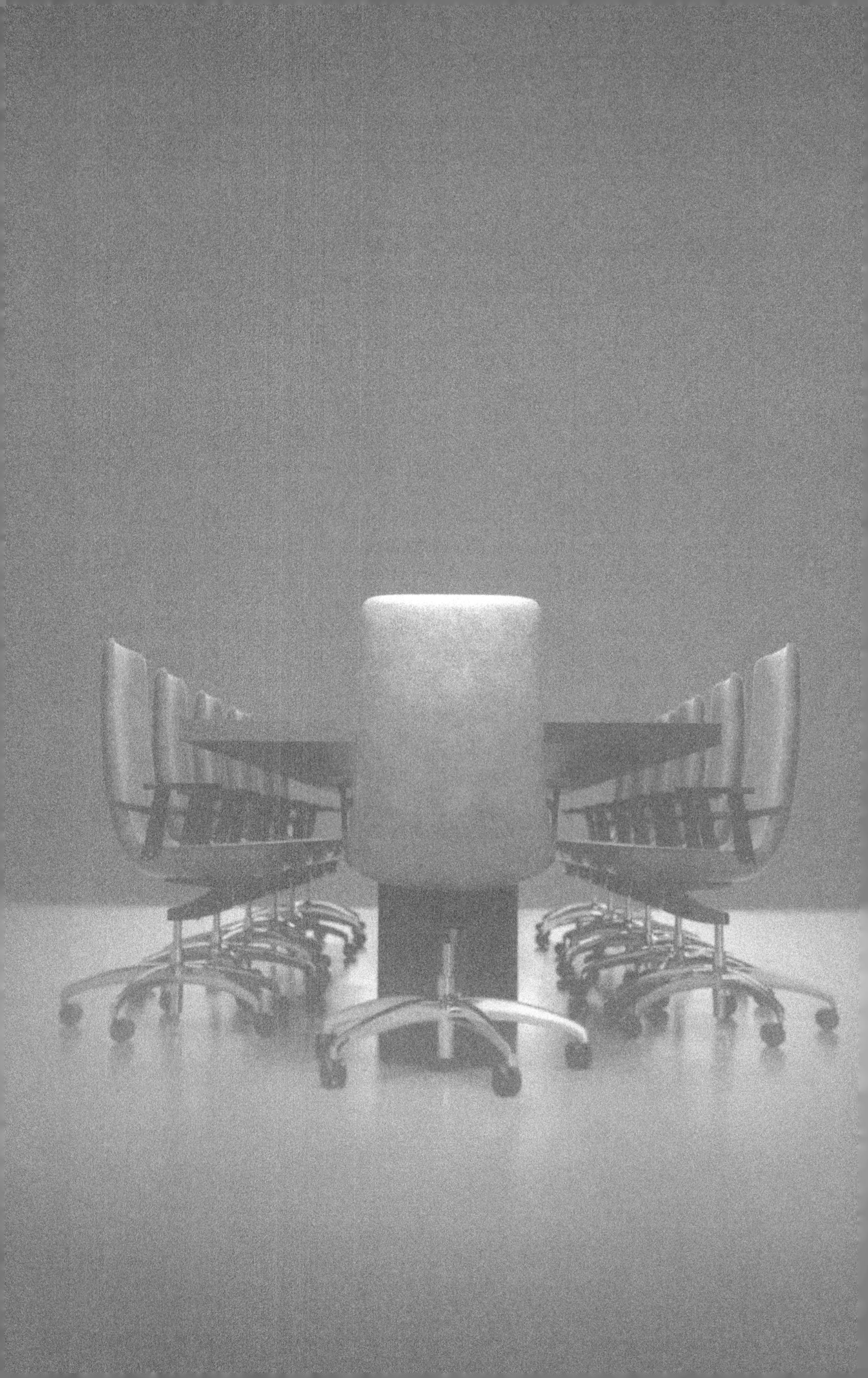

PART THREE

From Success to Significance

Bob Beauford used the term "from success to significance" almost thirty years ago when he wrote his book, *Halftime*. He was spot on. A friend referred me to the Halftime Institute's Fellows program when I found myself with an unanticipated dilemma. I had achieved my professional goals. I was in the C-Suite and doing board work … and yet I wanted more. Eventually, the day will come when all your hard work pays off and you finally get those keys to the C-Suite … at which point you might also find yourself asking, "Now what?" What do you want to do with your hard-earned experience and influence? Now that you know how to open doors, what doors would you like to see open? These last few chapters will help you look at the endless possibilities your future holds, with ideas on how to maximize them.

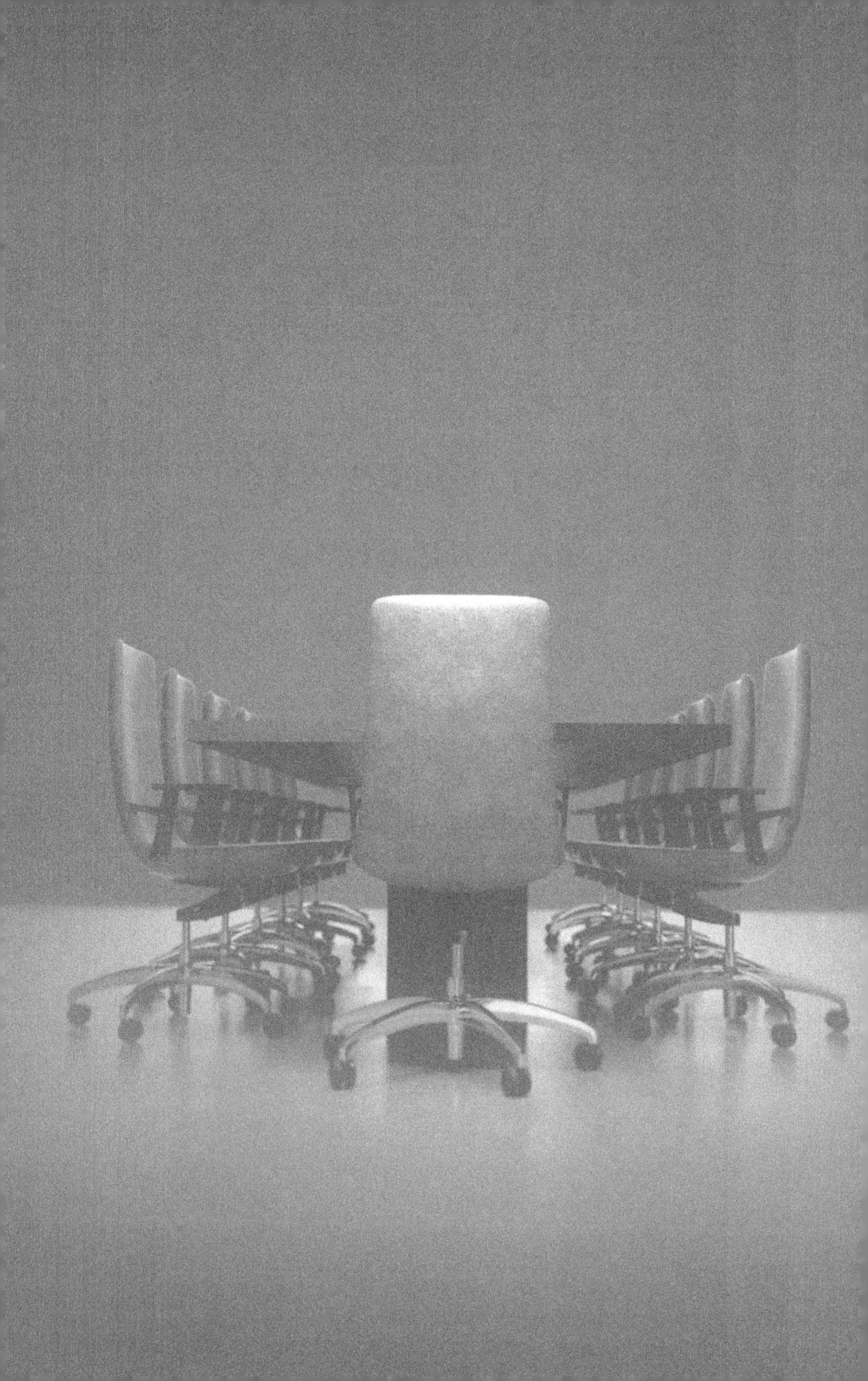

CHAPTER 12

Journey to the Boardroom

When I first started considering doing full-time board work, I had just left my last operating role at Informatica, and I didn't know how to go about filling out the rest of my board portfolio. I was on one public board, and then I was on two public boards, and I wanted to add another three or four board seats—that was my semiretirement plan. What was my strategy? I started talking to everyone with a pulse. I talked to every recruiter I had ever met, friends who were on boards, and people who had friends who were on boards. It was almost a full-time job, interviewing with all kinds of random companies. I was eager to fill out my board portfolio as quickly as possible.

In the middle of this process, a friend and mentor called me. He is a very successful business leader who works in venture capital, and he wanted to catch up. Of course, I immediately jumped on the phone. But my friend didn't want to talk about any boards he thought I might want to join.

Instead, he said, "Tracey, today I am doing an intervention with you."

Wait ... *what?*

"What in the world are you trying to achieve right now?" he went on to ask.

"Well," I started to explain, "I am recently retired, and I really want to add three to four new boards to my portfolio."

"Tracey, every company on the planet is doing back channel on you," he said with a laugh. "I am getting so many calls on 'Who is Tracey Newell?' And some of these companies aren't great companies ... so, again, what are you trying to accomplish?"

I repeated exactly what I had shared earlier: I really wanted to get on another three or four boards, and this was my semiretirement plan.

He said, "Tracey, you do not want to get three or four more board seats. You want one amazing board seat. I can get you on ten boards tomorrow with some bad companies. You need to slow down and get real clarity on what you truly want. And for the record, it will probably take you six months to find one great board seat."

(This sounds a lot like the approach to finding a great job, as we explored in the previous chapters, doesn't it?)

Today, whenever someone tells me they want help getting a board seat, I share this story. For board work, it's critical to be clear on what types of companies and CEOs you want to work with, even more so than when choosing a company to join as a full-time employee. Why? If you don't like a job, you can stay for a few years, and if you still aren't happy, you can make a change. Board seats don't work quite the same way. It's a longer-term commitment to the CEO, other board members, employees, and investors. If you're serious about building a presence in the boardroom, which I very much hope you are, it is not a commitment you should take lightly.

CHAPTER 12

What Happens in the Boardroom ...

Before I describe how boards work, I want to be clear that I'm concentrating on for-profit boards. Nonprofit boards can be easier for women to join, with women holding an average of 36–47 percent of seats on nonprofit boards, depending on the type of organization.[37] To be clear, nonprofit boards are critical—I have been (and am) involved with several nonprofit organizations, which I'll talk about a bit later. It is, however, the for-profit boardrooms where women are still underrepresented.

Work on a company board involves a significant commitment of time and effort, whether the company is public or privately owned. Boards provide oversight of management and operations, to include governance and compliance with laws and regulations, assessing risks, and safeguarding the company's assets. Board members contribute to the strategic direction of the company (my favorite area to focus on), providing insights and advice on growth opportunities, market positioning, and business development. They also provide financial oversight, reviewing and approving budgets, financial statements, and significant financial decisions, while monitoring the financial health of the company and ensuring accurate reporting. They are responsible for hiring, evaluating, and sometimes if required, changing the CEO, as well as assisting in succession planning. They're involved in communicating with stakeholders, crisis management, helping navigate significant transactions, and more.

So, how much time does this all take? As a board member, you will be responsible for attending regular board meetings, which can be held quarterly, bimonthly or even monthly. The meetings typically

---

37 "Nonprofit Boards Don't Resemble Rest of America," *NonProfit Times*, accessed September 12, 2024, https://thenonprofittimes.com/npt_articles/nonprofit-boards-dont-resemble-rest-america/.

last four to eight hours, but that doesn't include preparation time—reading documents and analyzing reports and financial statements—plus any necessary travel time. Many board members also serve on committees that meet separately from the full board, with the committees meeting quarterly at a minimum.

In other words, board work is a *job* in and of itself, although the scope of your workload will vary depending on the size and complexity of the company, as well as your specific responsibilities as a board member. All of which is why you should follow my friend's advice and take time to consider these factors and more when deciding which board seat to pursue.

Finding Your Perfect Match

Before you start looking for a board seat, you need to answer two basic questions, which are a lot like the questions you answered in your elevator pitch for an operating role:

1. What will you bring to the CEO, board, and management team? That is, who are you and how will you help this company succeed?

2. What does your perfect board seat look like? That is, what types of companies do you want to work with?

Let's start with the first question, getting clarity on what you're going to bring to the role as a board member. Ask yourself, Why would a CEO, a management team, and the rest of the board want you to join their board? What will you help them with? If a board wants me in the role, it's usually because the CEO wants someone on the team who has led high-growth sales, marketing, and customer success organizations. That's my background and what I bring to the table. When you're pursuing board work, it's important to think about what you bring to the table through the lens of the CEO and come up with three to five things you're confident you can help the company achieve during your term.

Once you're clear on what you have to offer, you're ready to think through which companies you want to focus on, which means it's time to go back to the spreadsheet we used in the last chapter to determine what sort of boards you want to serve on. The same kind of "frog-kissing" questions you asked while job hunting apply. Do you want to be on the board of a small company, or a larger one? A seat on the board of a smaller company will likely provide you with a more hands-on experience than the board of a large company. Private or public? Venture backed or private equity? Different corporate structures will result in different board experiences. I always look for an amazing CEO who can attract an A-team, a critical industry that is solving important problems, and a stellar product, but again, you may have a different "perfect profile." What matters is that you are very clear on your desired target.

Board members usually serve a two- to six-year term, with a three-year term being quite common for most companies. If the company is public, board members are elected; if it's private, you typically interview with the largest investors, the CEO, and other independent board members to be selected. Once your term is up, you are put up for election or approval again, and this is where the long-term commitment can really kick in. Once someone is on a board, it is very common that they are approved for a second term, as onboarding a new board member takes time. It is not uncommon to see a board member on the same board for six years or longer.

After following my friend's advice, I was able to win seats on the boards of a group of companies I'm deeply invested in. I have chosen to join boards where the CEO and management teams genuinely want board engagement (in an appropriate and helpful way, of course). I may be semiretired, but I still have a lot of energy to help my companies in any way I can. With that said, my personal belief is that if you're doing full-time board work, I would not try to balance more than four to six boards at one time. If you take on too many companies, calendar management can become a challenge as you align to other members' calendars. I was once told, "You don't want to be the difficult one when important meetings need to be scheduled with urgency." It was great advice.

At the beginning of this book, I shared some statistics on the shortage of women in the C-suite. It's even more challenging in the boardroom. According to the 50/50 Women on Boards Gender Diversity Index, the total percentage of women on corporate boards in the US was 28.4 percent as of December 2023. Here's how it breaks down by industry:

CONSUMER PRODUCTS AND RETAIL:
Highest representation, over 30 percent.

HEATHCARE:
Around 30 percent.

FINANCIAL SERVICES:
Close to 30 percent.

UTILITIES:
Approximately 25-30 percent.

TECHNOLOGY:
Around 20 percent.

INDUSTRIAL AND MANUFACTURING:
Close to 20 percent.

ENERGY AND MINING:
Just under 20 percent.

Clearly, we have a lot of work to do, but we also have a big opportunity. So, whatever you bring to the table, whatever you want from your board experience, the important thing is to do your homework, find the right board for you, and take your seat. We need you in there! My former colleague Alison Gleeson, who serves on a range of boards, has some thoughts to get you started.

TRANSFORMATIONAL LEADER: ALISON GLEESON, FORMER SENIOR VICE PRESIDENT AND BOARD MEMBER

Alison Gleeson, former Senior vice president of the Americas organization at Cisco, led the company's largest geographic region, managing over $25 billion in annual sales and overseeing nearly nine thousand employees across thirty-five countries. With more than twenty years at Cisco, she drove top-performing teams by emphasizing a customer-first approach, implementing go-to-market and data-driven strategies, and fostering strong partnerships. Alison is a recognized speaker on digital disruption, technology's role in business transformation, and empowering women in tech. Her commitment to professional development, inclusion, and diversity has earned her multiple accolades, including Connected World's Woman of IoT Award, Diversity Best Practices' Above and Beyond Legacy Award, and Michigan Council for Women in Technology's Woman of the Year Award. She served as Global executive sponsor and board president for Cisco's Connected Women's Network, supporting seven thousand members worldwide, currently serves on the board of directors for public companies Elastic, 8x8, and ZoomInfo, and is president of the Eli Broad College of Business's advisory board at Michigan State University, her alma mater.

***

One of my biggest regrets is that I took the advice of a colleague and did not accept a board position when it was offered to me while I was still an operator. I was worried it would be too much for me to handle due to my extensive travel, so I said no, and I regretted it almost immediately. The good news for you is I believe companies have evolved over the last five years, particularly with their support for female leaders, and many companies, especially in tech, sponsor board placement initiatives and encourage their female leaders to pursue board work.

The next time I was offered a spot on a board—this time the board of my alma mater, the Eli Broad Business School's advisory board at Michigan State University—I took it, and yes, I was still an operator at the time. That was my first board, and it was a really great experience, working alongside top business leaders across all industries and company sizes. It was a great entrée for me to see how a board works and get some experience. I've been on the Michigan State business school advisory board for over six years.

If you're interested in doing board work, here is my best advice:

1. **Get your first board seat while you're still an operator.** *You will be very much in learning mode during your first board position. If you're still in an operator role, you will have trusted advisors and a team around you to utilize and pull from. That's a much more conducive environment to be in when you are named to your first board seat.*

2. **Be deliberate.** *A lot of people ask me what the process is for getting on a board, and the reality is there is no process! So, if you really want to join a board, approach it seriously, give yourself a timeline, and leverage your network. It can take you a year or it can take you a month, but if you stick with it, you will get there.*

3. **Be prepared.** *Before I went on my first public board, I went through a training program where I hired a coach to train me on all the different committees, their missions, along with board responsibilities and duties. This allowed me to make informed decisions about which board position I wanted to pursue.*

Joining a corporate board is a great way to parlay the experiences you've gained over a long and successful career into a (literal) seat at the table. In our next chapter, we'll look at other ways to have significance, while we explore the idea of what you want your legacy to be over time.

CHAPTER 13

Leaving A Legacy

Ten to fifteen years ago, I started hearing this new whisper in my ear:

"Help me to do something that matters."

At this point, I was doing well in my career. I was achieving more than I had ever dreamed of, but at the same time, I wasn't quite sure what should come next. It was a bit like being at a football game when the game is half over and you're entering the second half. What did I want to do next? What was my strategy?

"Help me to do something that matters."

At first, I had no idea what that whisper was trying to tell me. I was in a big job, so I was arguably doing something that mattered. I was helping a ton of people—my employers, my employees, our customers, our shareholders. Why did I keep getting this feeling, tugging at my heartstrings, that it wasn't enough?

Then one day, it came to me. "I can do more to make a difference in helping people."

I felt called to do more. I yearned to do something impactful in more than a professional sense—something that wouldn't just make my boss happy, but rather something that would truly help tens of thousands of people. As I continued to sit with this feeling, a very specific prayer emerged from inside:

> **"Help me to do something that matters."**

"Help me to use the gifts that You've given me to make a difference in the lives of tens of thousands of people, people struggling from neglect, poverty and hopelessness."

That was it. That was the legacy I aspired to achieve. I simply needed a way to make it real. And as often happens, a way forward soon appeared, in the form of a very successful CEO and founder named Matt. (And yes, Matt is now an amazing friend.)

Matt introduced me to the book I referenced earlier titled *Halftime: Moving from Success to Significance*, by Bob Buford. It was a bestseller about thirty years ago, when people like Peter Drucker and Jim Collins shared that it was a must-read. In my opinion, it still is. Basically, the book's thesis is that the dreaded midlife crisis doesn't have to be a time of crisis at all. It can be a sort of reset point when you consider your strengths, what you like to do, and what matters to you and then shape the second half of your life around what you discover. It can be the gateway to a life of even greater significance. Which is what I had been looking for without realizing it.

Bob Buford was a Christian businessman who said, "My passion is to multiply all that God has given me, and in the process, give it back." The book was part of that giving back—it led to the creation of the Halftime Fellows program. While simplified, Bob's vision was to encourage successful leaders who were lucky enough to retire early to use the skills that made them so successful in the corporate world and apply them to the nonprofit world. It sounded ingenious to me. There is so much need in this world, and at the same time, there are so many people who know how to scale things. If you match the right person with the right project, they could really get big meaningful things done. The Halftime Fellows program became my road map as to how I wanted to spend time in my second half.

The Future beyond the Office

If you're an emerging leader, the second half of your life may feel very far away. I get it. We tend to be laser focused on our careers, especially in the early years. I certainly resembled this remark. At times I was barely surviving, between working at my overwhelming job and feeling overwhelmed with life. There were too many items on my to-do list and not enough of me to go around. But by my early forties, I started feeling a need to make a difference. When my kids were growing up, we joined the National Charity League, which is a nonprofit organization where moms and daughters serve together in local philanthropies. But I didn't have a master plan or vision regarding where I really want to spend my time making a difference longer term.

So, here's the thing. The same skills you're developing right now that are going to propel your journey to the C-suite and beyond are the kinds of skills nonprofits need to succeed in their missions to make the world a better place. I wish someone had helped me connect those dots when I was thirty or forty, instead of waiting until my inner voice wouldn't stop whisper-shouting at me. When I'm gone someday, I don't want people to think of me and say, "Oh, she had a great career." Life is short—the question to ask yourself is literally the old query: *What do you want on your tombstone?* What do you want your legacy to be? I want people to say that I made a difference in the world and that I helped people to reach their God-given potential.

Again, I'm not saying you need to figure all this out right now. What I am suggesting is that reaching the C-suite level gives you a lot of skills and can open a lot of doors as you move into the second half of your life. The fact that you may be in survival mode right now is not a reason to wait to at least ask yourself what you want to do with everything you've achieved over time. Only you can decide what you want your move from success to significance to look like. What do you want for your family, your community, your faith, your health? Do you have the desire to make a broader impact and leave a meaningful legacy? There's no right answer, but we only get one chance at life. So, let's talk about creating your future.

My Time in Halftime

Author T. D. Jakes wrote, "Your words will tell others what you think, but your actions will tell them what you believe."[38] After writing *Halftime*, Bob Buford kicked off the Halftime Fellows program. Halftime Fellows is a one-year structured program to help leaders design their personal road map, and yes, as I tend to do … *I signed up*. For me, the Halftime Fellows program helped me zero in on what kinds of actions I wanted to take. It helped me zero in on key questions to define my goals for my second half:

- What are my priorities personally, professionally and spiritually?

- What do I want to do to make a difference in serving others?

- How much time and capacity will I spend on each of these priorities?

---

38   T. D. Jakes, *He-Motions: Even Strong Men Struggle* (Putnam, 2004).

CHAPTER 13

- And so much more ...

The program offers many different ways to figure your goals and priorities out, including field trips to visit other Halftimers to see the good work they're doing, which I found incredibly inspiring. I became part of a community, meeting people who have gone through a similar journey to mine, participating in different programs to help me get clear about what I wanted to do. And for certain, I made new lifelong friendships that I will value deeply always. In the end, Halftime helped me decide that I want to use what I've learned over the course of my career to help others and connected me with opportunities to do that.

I have a girlfriend who describes the process as "chasing fireflies." The way she sees it, fireflies bring light to the world, and she's chasing lots of different projects that make the world a better and brighter place. I feel like I'm on a similar path, chasing a few fireflies of my own. Writing this book is one way for me to share what I've learned in my own journey with the intent to give back, helping women to accelerate their careers. I'm also very passionate about 4word, the Christian nonprofit I mentioned earlier that is also focused on helping women to reach their God-given potential. It's an amazing organization that has touched over four million women so far. Our goal is to reach ten million. I've recently joined the board and am very excited about where 4word is headed to make a difference in the lives of many.

I'm just as passionate about a nonprofit called Bridge2Rwanda (B2R), whose mission is to build a lifelong fellowship of high-capacity leaders in Africa to accelerate the growth of their countries and improve the lives of others. They also run a program called B2R Farms, which is focused on promoting Foundations for Farming and conservationist agriculture principles in order to eliminate food insecurity and reduce the impact of climate change. Because 85 percent of farmers in Rwanda are women trying to feed their families, there's a strong link to helping women here as well.

When you're going through the Halftime program, one of the questions you're asked is, "What makes you angry?" It has always made me angry that there are people in this world who don't know how they're going to feed their children, who don't have the right to clean water, whose children don't have the right to education … how is that possible in today's world? Halftime put me in touch with Dale Dawson, the CEO of B2R. I talked with him about what he was doing, and somehow, our meeting turned into a two-hour conversation. At the end, I said, "So Dale, what you're doing is amazing. But why are you talking with a software executive from the Silicon Valley? How can I help you? I don't know anything about farming or Rwanda."

He smiled and said, "I think I need help in all kinds of ways. Come to Rwanda and we'll figure it out."

I had just gotten home from a two-week-long, overseas trip with my husband. The trip that Dale wanted me to join was literally three weeks out. And, I have to be honest—jumping on a plane to fly twenty hours to the other side of the world each way was not extremely appealing. I simply did not want to go to Rwanda. But that's not what I told Dale. I told Dale I was going to pray about it.

And I did. I said, "God, I really don't want to go to Rwanda, but if you want me to go to Rwanda, I will do it. But none of this whisper stuff … punch me in the nose and tell me to go."

Around this same time, I had signed up with a new Bible study group at my new church, and the leader of the study called me and said, "Hey, there's a women's retreat this weekend—would you be willing to come?" Again, my initial thought was, "I just got home! I don't want to go to a retreat; I won't know anyone!" But I also had this niggling feeling saying, *What's your problem? This wonderful woman is asking you to go to a retreat; just go to the retreat* ...

I went, and honestly, it was terrific. The topic for the retreat was Psalm 23, and all Friday night and Saturday, compelling speakers (pastors from all over the US) were giving their take on the psalm. It was literally a Ted Talks for pastors, and I loved it. But there was only one leader who did not talk about Psalm 23 ...

He was a pastor from Rwanda talking about the genocide.

For certain, hearing Rwanda mentioned in the middle of several Ted Talks on Psalm 23 caught my attention. It was certainly off topic, and it piqued both my interest and compassion for such a horrendous tragedy. However, it wasn't enough to get me to fly forty hours in a ten-day period. It was more of a whisper than a punch in the nose.

So, I called my friend Kim, who was my only friend who had traveled to Rwanda, to ask her advice. I told her that I had met Dale, who was the CEO of the nonprofit called Bridge2Rwanda. Before I could get too far, she said, "Tracey, I know Dale. I adopted my son through Bridge2Rwanda."

"You did what?" I asked. If this was a coincidence, then it was a big one.

Kim then asked me if I wanted to talk to her friend who had been very engaged with the country of Rwanda for years. I of course said yes—I could not wait to meet her.

As I jumped on the call, this new contact greeted me with, "Tracey, I've heard your name five times this week from all sorts of different people, and I've never met you. What do you want to know?" We had a great conversation, and when we finished, she asked me if I had any other questions for her.

I did. "I'm trying to decide whether I should go on this trip or not, because I really don't want to go."

She didn't hesitate, "Buy a plane ticket and don't look back."

I'd asked for guidance, and it was given. And saying yes to Rwanda is one of the best decisions I have ever made.

B2R Farms has trained over forty thousand farmers in Rwanda on how to increase their farming output by one hundred to two hundred percent their traditional yield (remember—these are farmers trying to feed their families!). B2R is having great impacts in both education and solving for the digital divide, while also working to literally put a dent in world hunger. There is a saying in Africa that while today Africa cannot feed itself, tomorrow it could feed the world, and many of Rwanda's neighboring countries are paying close attention to the results of this program. I am honored to be a part of it. And yes, I'm having a blast.

I don't mean to in any way imply I didn't have fun in my career. I absolutely loved what I did and remain humbled by the talented teams I was so grateful to work with and for. But serving nonprofits for me is a completely different kind of fun, and I am grateful for any help I can provide along the way.

Find Your Passion

If you're ready to find your own opportunity to give back, I'm excited to help you get started. First, ask yourself a few questions: *What am I passionate about? What am I angry about?* That's what led me to B2R and 4word. *Are there things I used to be excited about that I've let go of or forgotten?* The answers to these questions will point you in the direction of the issues that matter to you, what you like to do, and where you can make a real difference.

Of course, I recommend the Halftime Fellows program as a great resource to start this journey of figuring out how you might get involved and make an impact. And you don't have to want to change the world to benefit from what Halftime has to offer. More than anything, it's a great resource to help you gain clarity around what your priorities are for the second half of your life, whatever they might be, along with some help in making those things a reality. I've met Halftime fellows whose mission is to spend as much time as possible with their grandchildren as they pour into future generations. I've met others who have written books and built coaching programs, while others built large nonprofits. The community—talking to people who have gone through a similar time of reflection to make a difference in the world—was hugely impactful and helpful.

How to get started? Once you have a few ideas, take a baby step and try something that appeals to you. Call a local nonprofit or church that you're interested in and ask what they have coming up. Volunteer at an event where they need some help, just one time; it doesn't have to be a major commitment. Then ask yourself, *Did I like it? Did I not like it? If I did like it, what was it about the experience that appealed to me?* Over time, you will see a path emerge, and you can follow it to more opportunities that resonate with you. Getting there will be half the fun, as you learn new things and meet new people along the way.

And as a reminder, planning your legacy isn't only about deciding which charities to get involved with. Writing this book has been part of Halftime for me, because writing is something I used to dream about. When I was young, I was a voracious reader, and I loved to write. I recently reread some stories I wrote when I was in fifth grade, and I thought, *Darn, for fifth grade … that was pretty good.* But I had completely lost that side of myself. Halftime reminded me and helped me to reconnect with this part of myself. However you get there, my hope is that you, too, will spend time thinking through what brings you joy and what you want your legacy to look like longer term and explore what you want to achieve in your second half.

TRANSFORMATIONAL LEADER: DIANE ADAMS, CHIEF CULTURE AND TALENT OFFICER AT SPRINKLR

Diane Adams is the chief culture and talent officer at Sprinklr, where she oversees human resources, talent acquisition, and the employee experience. For over twenty years, Adams has built and led high-performance, values-driven cultures at both private and public companies. At Cisco, she played a pivotal role in growing the company from 3,800 to over 70,000 employees, driving key talent strategies during a period of exponential growth. She later served as chief people officer at Allscripts, Qlik Technologies, and McGraw-Hill Education, where she led cultural transformations and strengthened employee engagement. Adams is also committed to giving back through various leadership and mentoring initiatives. She serves as Director Emeritus of the International Breakthrough T1D organization (previously JDRF), where she was recognized with the "Living and Giving" award due to her contributions. She also serves Communities in Schools of North Carolina, the Durham Rescue Mission, and the Greater Raleigh Chamber of Commerce, supporting causes related to education, health, and economic growth. Additionally, she is an advisor to BrightPlan, Betterworks, Outlier Health, and Semper-

CHAPTER 13

Virens Ventures, which focuses on investments in health and wellness startups.

***

I feel very fortunate that giving back started early in my career. When I was in my thirties, an uncle referred me to serve on the Wake County Housing Authority Board. At the time, I knew nothing about affordable housing or the struggles these people faced. The more I was involved, the more I learned and the more perspective I gained. The role was extremely fulfilling.

Then my youngest daughter, Danielle, was diagnosed with Type 1 diabetes at only four years old. I joined the North Carolina (JDRF) board and later the international board, and discovered that my strength was in fundraising. JDRF's annual walks and galas have become a family affair—or a friends-and-family affair. Because my jobs have been global, I have friends all around the world, and they all know this cause is important to me. They know because for the first few years after Danielle's diagnosis, she had seizures, so I never left her at home. She traveled with me and sat at the back of the HR meetings, leadership meetings…she just was there.

The entire community surrounded us. Every year, we'd bring at least a hundred new grads to Raleigh, and every year, those new grads would do a fundraiser for diabetes and raise a hundred thousand dollars. One year they rented out a bar and formed a band, and I'll never forget nine-year-old Danielle standing up on that stage singing "Keep on Believing."

All these years it's been such a part of our life, the walks and the galas and working alongside our community—we've realized people are so important to us. We're fortunate to be surrounded by family and friends who also want to make a difference, and I'm fortunate to be able to make a difference as a volunteer for other causes that matter to me.

When it comes to your own move from success to significance, my advice is as follows:

1. **Get involved now.** *You don't need to wait until you're higher on the ladder to join a nonprofit board or committee. Getting involved while you're still early in your career gives you an opportunity to make a bigger difference not just beyond your career, but in it. My volunteer work has deepened my perspective, my relationships, my network, my knowledge, everything. It's made me a better leader.*

2. **Bring people with you**. *Engage your family and your friends, but also your teams. Remember, you are a role model for others, showing them what leadership looks like, and also helping them to have greater perspective. Influence is a key skill we all need to develop, and that ability to communicate and inspire people to join with you is key.*

3. **Show up for others and their causes.** *When I think about leadership and being all in it with people, and the way people have shown up for me and my family, it only makes sense to pay it forward. People never forget how you make them feel. And when you ask people their story and learn their why, it grows your perspective, which makes you a much greater leader.*

For most people, figuring out what to do with their second half involves trying a lot of different things in order to discover what moves them, what resonates, what they want to devote their time to. The important thing is to start thinking and reflecting about your road map now, even if you don't have a great deal of time to execute these plans today. When you're finally ready to launch into your second half, you won't be caught flat footed.

In our next and final chapter, we'll take a closer look at something I've hinted at, especially in this chapter, but haven't really elaborated on—the connection between work and faith.

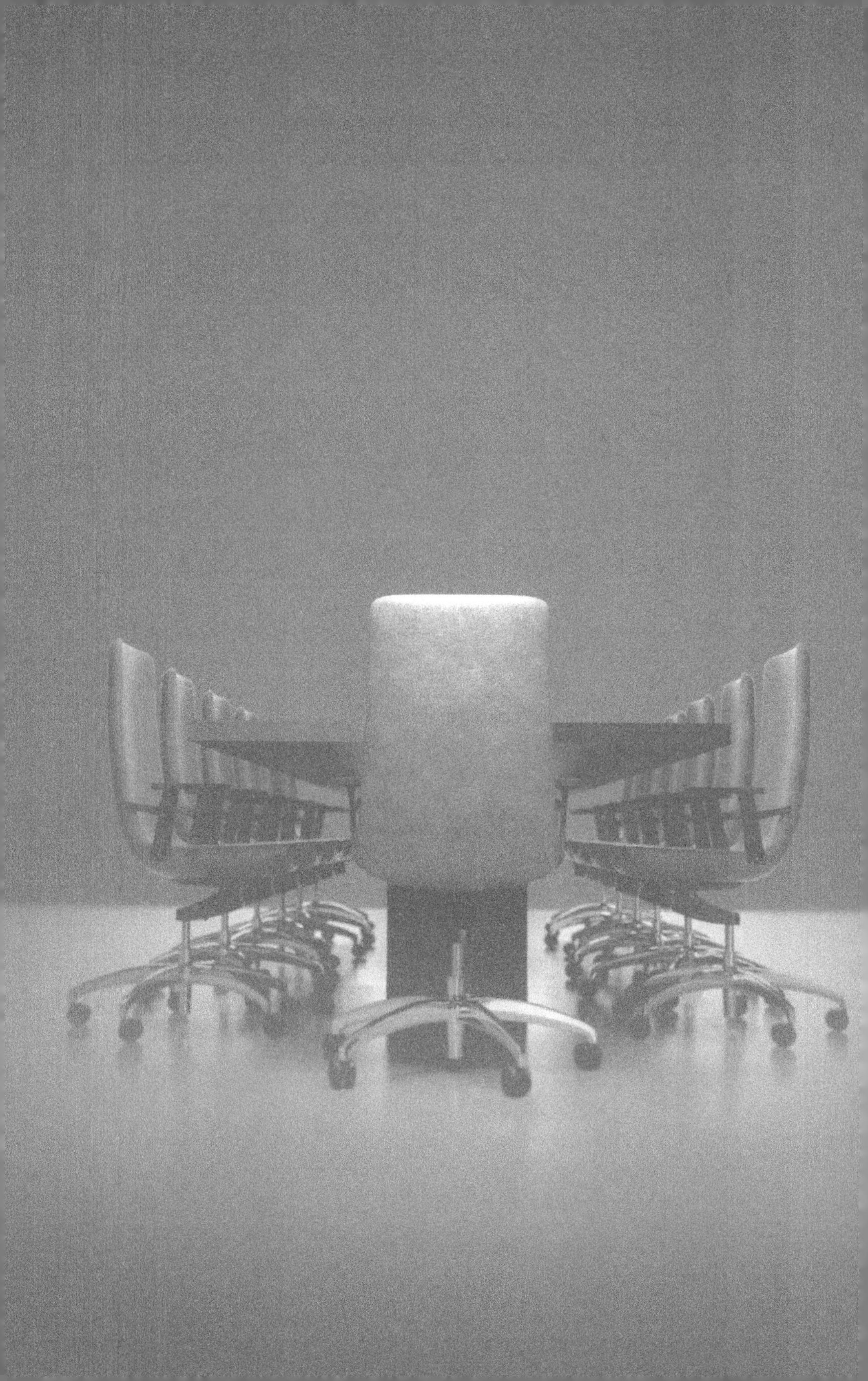

CHAPTER 14

Faith and Your Career

Between 4word, B2R, the Halftime Foundation, and all the references to prayer, I've dropped more than a few hints throughout this book that faith is an important part of who I am. It may have left you wondering, "Is she *really* going to go there?" Faith and career are a bit like church and state, right? You're not supposed to talk about things like your belief in God in a book about work!

In my mind that isn't the case. God has had a huge impact on not just my personal life, not just my character, not just my belief system, but also on my career. They are, for me, inseparable. So, in this final chapter, I want to take a closer look at the intersection between faith and career, and what that looks like for me, and what it might look like for you.

I've always leaned heavily on my faith throughout my life, and even more so when I needed direction. In the last chapter, I shared the story of discovering B2R and how it took a few acts of faith to get me to the point where I could commit to an organization that I am now extremely passionate about. Like many leaders, when I need to make important decisions, personally or professionally, I pray for guidance. I recall one specific time when I felt strongly that I needed to make a career change and that my next role had to be the right one. I was at a crossroads and very much in need of guidance.

So, I started praying about it. I would pray all the time. I'd be out for a walk or a hike and say, "God, you know me. I am not always the best at listening. I know I should listen for Your whisper, but I don't always hear that whisper. So, I need you to make it obvious, with people that I trust, on which job I should take." (Yes, this is very much like my prayer on whether to go to Rwanda; praying for direction has been a big part of my life.)

I got to the point where I knew there was one specific company I really wanted to join, and in the spirit of following my own advice of talking myself out of the job, I called a friend who I have a lot of respect for and asked what he thought about it. I told him, "This is what I think I'm going to do."

He sighed and said, "Oh, really? Well, yeah, it is okay ..."

I immediately deflated. I was so excited about this job, and I thought he would be too. So, I asked, "Why is it just okay?"

He told me he "guessed" the company was a good company but shared that the market category was "a bit challenging." He went on to add, "I mean, it is software as a service, which is cool." This was not the glowing review I was looking for.

Now it was my turn to sigh. This was not at all what I wanted to hear. But I asked him, "Okay, well what is important right now?"

He came back with three words:

Advanced persistent threat. APT.

This was a cybersecurity term, which was fairly new at the time. I painstakingly wrote it down very carefully. Advanced Persistent Threat. APT. Got it. My friend explained what it was, that this new thing called "ransomware" was on the rise, and why it was an exciting new market in cybersecurity. He also told me that, at the time, the hot company in this space was known as FireEye. Given this new information, I knew I couldn't take the job at the company I was leaning into.

So, I called the recruiter back. I said, "I can't take this job because I'm not convinced that this company is differentiated enough." The recruiter replied, "Tracey, you need to spend more time with the CEO and understand his vision, so I'm going to set up time for you to do one last meeting with him."

I sat down with the CEO, and he immediately jumped on the whiteboard. Regarding my suddenly cold feet, he said, "You're asking the right questions." And then he said, "Let me tell you where we're going …

"We're getting into this new space." And on the whiteboard of the conference room we were sitting in, he wrote in big letters … *Advanced Persistent Threat.*

He went on to share, "And we're going to compete with this company. Its name is FireEye."

I literally looked up and said, "Thank you." Of course, I took the job.

The decision to join this company changed the trajectory of my career and my life.

Now don't get me wrong, I don't in any way mean to imply that life always works this way. I believe that God—just like any good parent—does not give us everything we want when we want it. Our timing is often wrong, and what we want isn't always right. But my faith in *asking for guidance* and *being willing to listen* when making important personal and professional decisions has been a big part of my journey. I know I would not be where I am today without my faith.

Faith, Work, and You

In my experience, my faith and career have fit together seamlessly. I imagine a person could face a time in their career where they're asked to do something that they know is absolutely wrong because it's against their integrity and their ideals, but then again, if that happened to me, I'd probably question why I was working for that company in the first place, and you probably would too. Even without my faith, I always say integrity is table stakes. If you don't have it, we cannot work together. While Christianity teaches us to turn the other cheek, be kind to each other, and do the right thing, I also feel like that's just part of what good and decent people do every day.

Since that's the case, you might be asking why I'm crossing the unbreakable line in discussing my faith with you, never mind bringing it to the office in the first place. For me, it comes back to the author C. S. Lewis. He said, "Christianity, if false, is of no importance, and if true, of infinite importance. The only thing it cannot be is moderately important." He went on to share, "We must show our Christian colors if we are to be true to Jesus Christ."[39] So that is what I try to do in everything I do, including my work.

I love the story of Lynsi Snyder, the thirty-seven-year-old CEO of the California fast-food chain In-N-Out Burger. If you know anything about the company, which was founded by her grandfather, it's that their burgers are wait-in-line-around-the-block legendary—and if you know anything else, it may be that, when you order one of those amazing burgers, a shake, or a soft drink, if you peer really closely at the cup or the wrapper, you'll see a Bible verse discreetly printed right on it. Snyder has recently expanded that practice by adding more verses to more of the chain's products. As she shared with *Christianity*

---

39 C. S. Lewis, *Mere Christianity* (HarperOne, 2001)

Today magazine, "I finally found that the deep need in my heart can only be filled by Jesus and my identity in Him." That means serving burgers with a side of inspiration.[40]

Now, I get that you probably work for a company that is not going to allow you to print Bible verses on hundreds of thousands of paper products. I also get that the simple act of talking about faith can be pretty intimidating in a secular workplace. Again, church and state! Lines will be crossed! I say, *go ahead and cross them*. Although to get started, you really don't have to do much at all. Jesus is very clear in his commandments to love thy neighbor as thyself. So, show up in the workplace modeling what He asked of us: be kind, be there, be present, be helpful, practice servant leadership, be all those things. Showing up as your best possible self is one foolproof way to marry your work to your faith.

Still, there are things you can do that are a bit more deliberate. Right now, there's a lot of energy behind bringing our "authentic selves" to the workplace instead of trying to conform to some universal norm. There are so many ways to bring your authentic self to work as a person of faith. We have already spent time discussing praying for guidance in your work life as well as your personal life. I used to frequently wear a necklace with a cross on it to work. You can show your faith through your actions—I once heard from a very successful attorney who told me that whenever he heard someone in his firm was having a hard time, rather than saying, "I will pray for you," he looked them in the eye and said, "I am so sorry. *May* I pray for you and your family?" This way he received buy-in, and the people he offered to

---

40 Michelle Gant, "Why Does In-N-Out Print Bible Verses on Its Cups and Wrappers?," *Today*, October 9, 2019, https://www.today.com/food/why-does-n-out-print-bible-verses-its-cups-wrappers-t164235.

pray for remembered him as someone who genuinely helped them get through a difficult time.

Sharing your faith with your coworkers doesn't have to be awkward. It certainly should not be forceful, because talking about your faith isn't being forceful—if it's who you are, it's being normal. For example, if you're asked the very normal question "What did you do this weekend?" and you went to church, it would be a very normal thing for you to share that information. It's also a great opportunity to perhaps invite your coworker to join you sometime.

> **Sharing your faith with your coworkers doesn't have to be awkward.**

There are actually some interesting statistics on this topic. According to Thom Rainer's book *The Unchurched Next Door*,[41] 82 percent of our friends and family who don't attend church are at least somewhat likely to come to church if they're invited. And there's more. Rainer's book also reveals that seven out of ten unchurched people *have never been invited to church in their whole lives*! This statistic crushed me as a believer. *Come on, people! We can do better!* And for our final Transformational Leader, I'd like to introduce someone who is "doing better": Diane Paddison.

---

41 Thom S. Rainer, "*The Unchurched Next Door: Understanding Faith Stages as Keys to Sharing Your Faith*" (Zondervan, 2003).

CHAPTER 14

TRANSFORMATIONAL LEADER: DIANE PADDISON, GLOBAL EXECUTIVE, FOUNDER, 4WORD

Diane Paddison, 4word founder, is a Harvard MBA, former global executive of two Fortune 500 companies—CBRE and ProLogis—and one Fortune 1000 company—Trammell Crow Company—and currently serves as an independent director for two corporate and two not-for-profit boards. As a leading advocate for Christian women in the workplace. Diane published *Work, Love, Pray* in 2011, which laid the foundation for 4word, along with *Be Refreshed: A Year of Devotions for Women in the Workplace* in 2017. She authors weekly posts at 4wordwomen.org and has been a featured columnist for the *Washington Times*, and the 4word Mentor Program has been highlighted in the *Wall Street Journal's* MarketWatch.

***

I was on the global executive teams of two Fortune 500 companies and one Fortune 1000 company, and in every case, I was the only woman. I wanted to be a part of changing that picture. When I was in my forties, I gathered a community of four other women of faith, all professionals, all moms, all either married or who had been married, and we talked about things we didn't talk about with anyone else. I felt like there had to be other women who needed this kind of community, but when I did the research, I found twelve hundred marketplace ministries led by men, or for men, or for men and women. When I looked for global marketplace ministries led by women for women, I found zero. I shared this with my mentor, Bob Buford, and he said, "I know you can build organizations. You have got to start this organization, and you need to write a book." So, I did.

Thirteen years later, 4word has grown to the point where we serve four million women around the globe through digital content like podcasts, live and virtual community groups, and a mentor program that has so far paired close to nine hundred mentees with professional women leaders. Ninety-eight percent of our mentees say that because of their shared faith, they're able to go very deep very quickly because they have a common language. We've seen lives change dramatically.

If you're trying to balance your faith and your career, here is my advice:

1. **Know your priorities.** *For me, it's my faith, my family, then my work. When I would consider a move for a job, I would always ask, "Are they going to support me in what I believe in?" Make sure you're really diligent about researching and thinking about decisions you make to ensure that they match.*

2. **Build your network including like-minded people ...** *I am very intentional about my network including Christian leaders that I respect. Of course, I have friends and colleagues who I love and respect tremendously who do not share my faith, but 90 percent of my network that I keep in touch with regularly is made up of people who do.*

3. **... Especially your mentors and sponsors.** *If they don't share the same faith and priorities as you do, a mentor or sponsor,*

CHAPTER 14

however well intentioned, might guide you in a direction that does not fit with your priorities.

The main reason my faith has been so important to me and that I chose to include it in this book is that this can be a tough world. Even for those of us who are privileged to be able to chase our dreams, never mind wake up every day with food, clean water, and a roof over our heads, life can still be hard. And while Christ never promised that life was going to be easy, he did share, "Come to Me, all you who labor and are heavy laden, and I will give you rest. Take My yoke upon you, and learn from Me, for I am gentle and lowly in heart, and you will find rest for your souls. For My yoke is easy, and My burden is light" (Matt. 11:28–30 [NKJV]). I can't imagine not having that support when life pushes me down.

I'm very grateful that in good times and bad times, I was always grounded in the knowledge that I wasn't, ever, by myself. Many know the famous poem "Footprints in the Sand," where the writer describes walking along a beach with God, seeing two sets of footprints in the sand, except during the difficult times in their life, when they notice only one set of footprints. The writer questions God, asking why He would abandon him at the hardest time. And God replies, "That's when I was carrying you."

I really believe that. And I honestly believe, with every ounce of my being, that I could never have gotten where I am today without my faith and without God carrying me through those hard times.

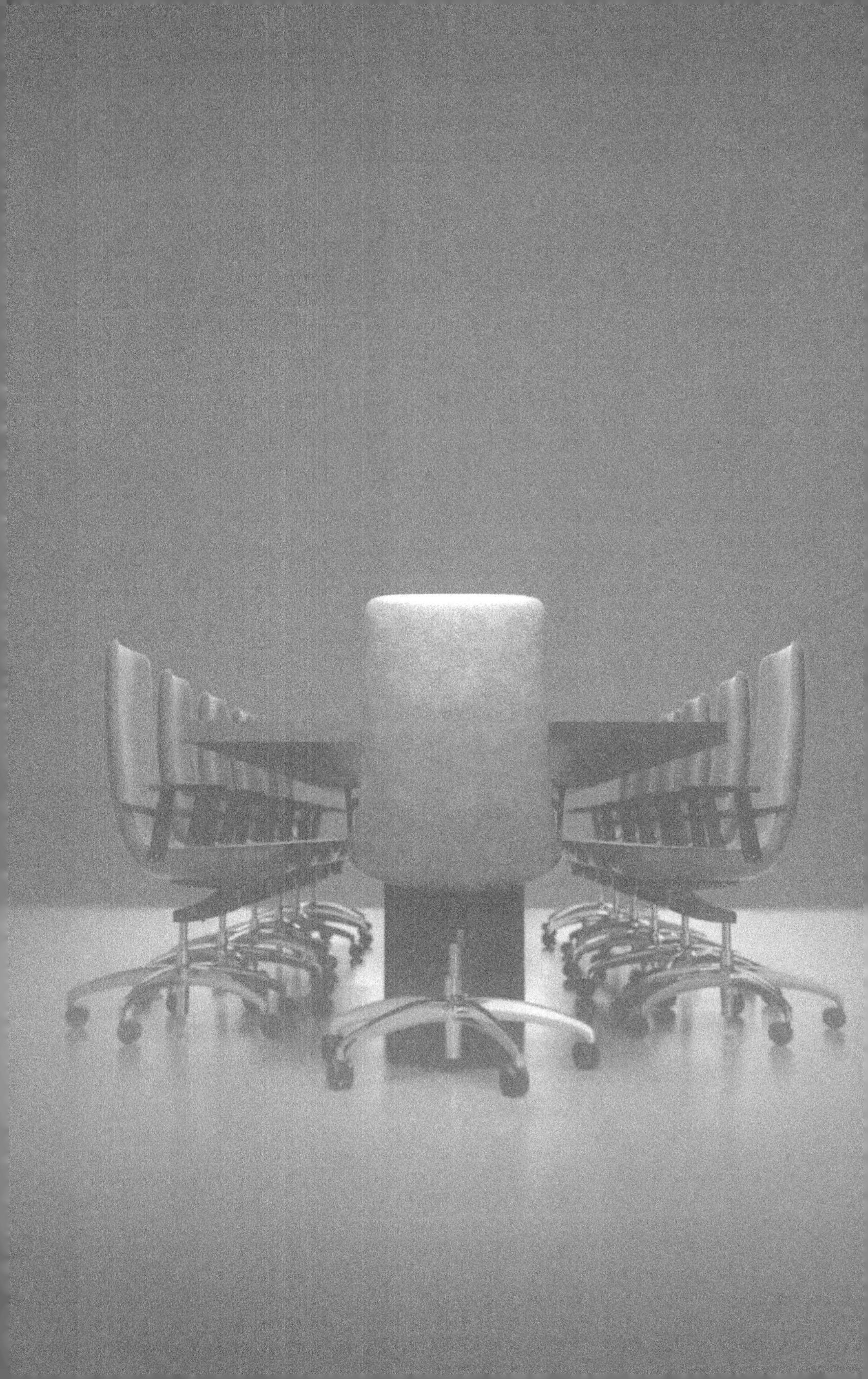

CONCLUSION

When I think about how far I've come in my career, I can't help but think back to the very beginning, which happened at the start of my senior year at UC Santa Barbara. It is a ridiculous story; I wasn't trying to start a career of any kind at the time. My intention was to graduate and go to law school, becoming a lawyer like my father. But at this point I was on campus two weeks early before my senior year began. I was bored and also broke, which may have contributed to the boredom factor. And suddenly I saw an ad in the school paper looking for someone to sell AT&T telephone calling cards, five days a week for five dollars per hour.

Now, if you are under forty, you probably have no idea what a "calling card" is. Back in the days before cellphones, the primary way college students talked to their friends and family back home was via a pay phone, and to use a pay phone, you needed change—specifically, quarters. We were constantly scouring the couch cushions for change, walking around with pockets full of quarters jangling whenever we wanted to talk to anyone. *(I promise this is actually true ... you can google it if you don't believe me!)*

Anyway, I called the 800 number in New Jersey and told the woman on the other end, "Hey, I'll take this job. I'll take my $200 per week."

The woman on the other end had a different plan in mind. She said, "No, no. We need someone to run the program and hire ten to fifteen kids at your university."

I said no. I was a senior in college; I didn't want this responsibility. Managing people was not in my future.

But she insisted. "This is a pilot program in a dozen universities, and we really *need* someone to run it."

A voice in my head said, "There's no way I can (or want to) manage all of these college kids."

But that's not what I said to the woman on the phone. I said, "Fine, I'll take the job."

This may have been the first of what you now know are many instances of me replying to that voice in my head that says *you can't* to get it to go away.

Part of the job was putting together a sales team, so I had to beg, plead, and whine until I somehow convinced fifteen of my closest friends (all seniors) to stand with me in front of the University Center and try to convince our fellow students to sign up for these calling cards. It was, without question, the worst job in the world. It was not that these calling cards were a bad product. But calling cards were new back then, so no one understood what we were selling, and no one wanted to take time out of their day to listen to me or one of my friends extol the (very real!) virtues of our product.

It was a disaster. We were not making money. The recruiter hadn't exactly spelled out the fine print, which was that we would be paid commission of one dollar per card sold; the five-dollars-per-hour "salary" was based upon us hypothetically selling five cards an hour.

Which was not happening. After two days perched in our spots in front of the student center, we were miserable. We hated our job. I looked at my friends and said, "There's got to be a better way."

Then I asked, "What do college kids want?"

They all said beer.

I said, "We can't give away beer on campus. What else do they want?"

They all said food. Bingo.

I went down to this little shop that sold cookies and asked the kid at the counter what their cheapest cookie was. He said, "Well, our day-olds are twenty-five cents."

I asked, "How many do you have?"

"I don't know," he said. "Fifty? A hundred? How many do you want?" I took them all.

The next time my friends and I took our spots in front of the student center, we offered a free cookie to anyone who (a) listened to our spiel about the calling card and (b) actually signed up. Our sales went crazy. At the end of the two-week pilot period, AT&T called and asked, "What is going on in Santa Barbara?" I told them we were just running their program. They said, "Well, you can run it all year."

So I did, and it was fun. I loved solving problems and thinking of a different way to build a better mousetrap. I loved the model of helping people, and I really loved being paid for my performance. The harder I worked, the more I was rewarded. I think it's true for most careers, but seeing my performance translate into actual dollars really resonated with me.

Needless to say, I never became a lawyer.

Still, when I graduated in 1988, the economy was tough. Nobody could get a job. But I now had a foothold in the door with AT&T. I called them relentlessly. I was so desperate, I literally stalked the recruiters, calling them every single day until they finally interviewed me for a sales job. I didn't even know what that was really ... nobody in my family worked in sales (although technically I had been in sales for an entire school year). They offered me the position, and when they did, they put me on speakerphone, and all the recruiters I'd been pestering nonstop cheered. I went to work for AT&T, a terrific company that prepared me for my career leading sales and marketing teams.

When I look back at this story, I can see the seeds of the person I am today in so much of what I achieved, even though at the time it felt as though everything happened almost by accident. I was presented with a problem, I found a solution, I ensured people I liked became involved, we all had fun solving the problem at hand—and we got paid. I didn't need an Ivy League MBA for any of this to happen, and, as it turned out, I didn't need those things to move from the University Center at UCSB to the C-suite and the boardroom.

And neither do you.

Everything you need to get where you want to go is already inside you. My hope is that you now have a better idea of how to tap into the gifts you've been given and make the most of them. Stay open to learning, to growing, to doing a little planning, to building strong relationships, and yes, to working really hard, and who knows how far you can go?

When my kids were small—ten, twelve, thirteen years old—they started giving me presents for Mother's Day and my birthday. There would be a pair of socks, a calendar, a little chart, or a poster, but they always said the same thing. *She believed she could, so she did.* The first few times I received one of these gifts, I burst into tears. They got it. My kids understood what I was trying to teach them—that all of

Everything you need to get where you want to go is already inside you.

this wasn't for me; it was for them. I wanted them to know that they could do this too. They could accomplish great things, just like they believed that I could.

As author Marianne Williamson shares, "Who are you not to be brilliant, gorgeous, talented, and fabulous?" Who are you not to be a board member or a CEO? Whether you're a believer or not, you, too, are a child of God. And the whole world is waiting for you to step into your greatness.

I cannot wait to see all that you will achieve.

ACKNOWLEDGMENTS

I cannot thank enough the stellar women and role models who are featured as the Transformational Leaders highlighted throughout this book. I am eternally grateful for your friendship, for lessons learned from each of you, and for your countless hours of dedication in accelerating the success of the next generation of women leaders.